All 'Bout Canada

A COMPENDIUM OF CANADIANA

ELIZABETH F. HILL

Art by ALEX MACASKILL

NIMBUS
PUBLISHING
NIMBUS.CA

Nimbus Publishing Limited
3660 Strawberry Hill Street, Halifax, NS, B3K 5A9
(902) 455-4286 nimbus.ca

Printed and bound in Canada

NB1466

Art direction: Heather Bryan & Whitney Moran
Cover design and illustrations: Alex MacAskill, Midnight Oil Print & Design House
Editor: Marianne Ward
Proofreader: Angela Mombourquette
Interior design: Jenn Embree

Library and Archives Canada Cataloguing in Publication

Title: All 'bout Canada : a compendium of Canadiana / Elizabeth F. Hill.
Other titles: All about Canada
Names: Hill, Elizabeth F., 1958- author.
Description: Features dictionary-style entries and a poem for each letter in the alphabet. | Includes bibliographical references.
Identifiers: Canadiana (print) 20200164929 | Canadiana (ebook) 20200164937 | ISBN 9781771088602 (softcover) | ISBN 9781771088619 (HTML)
Subjects: LCSH: Canada—Miscellanea. | LCSH: Canada—History—Miscellanea. | LCSH: Canada—Poetry. | LCSH: Canada—History—Poetry.
Classification: LCC FC60 .H55 2020 | DDC 971.002—dc23

Nimbus Publishing acknowledges the financial support for its publishing activities from the Government of Canada, the Canada Council for the Arts, and from the Province of Nova Scotia. We are pleased to work in partnership with the Province of Nova Scotia to develop and promote our creative industries for the benefit of all Nova Scotians.

For Mom, Debbie, and Robin

Eh?

Zed

Acknowledgements

THIS BOOK WOULD NEVER HAVE BEEN COMPLETED WITHOUT MY EARLY CRITICS, who found the time to read the first draft and to provide me with such inspirational comments as: "What a fun book!" "It's not as bad as you think!" "I'm proud of you!" "I really hate this type of book and I didn't want to read it, but I actually got interested!" "You sure didn't put a lot of effort into *this* entry!" You know which comment belongs to you: Robin Hill, Rita Marler, Debbie Okun-Hill, Patricia Olafson, and Elizabeth Sheppard. My thanks and my love.

It has been a pleasure and a privilege to work with the friendly and extremely competent staff at Nimbus Publishing. A special thank you to my wonderful editor, Marianne Ward, for your good humour, endless patience, and insightful comments and suggestions. I really do hope we can meet up in a national park!

A IS AURORA BOREALIS AT NIGHT,
WHICH SHIVERS AND SHIMMERS
   WITH EERIE GREEN LIGHT

ACES, ANNE, ASTRONAUTS, ANIK A-1,
ACADIANS, ATWOOD, AND ANDERSON

Canadians often call *aurora borealis* the "northern lights." These are caused when solar winds—streams of charged particles (ions) from the sun—interact with the earth's magnetic field. Some Inuit call aurora "aqsarniit" (football players), said to be spirits of the dead who are playing football with a walrus skull. (The football game might be a traditional Inuit game called akraurak or aqijut. In this game, two lines of players face each other and kick a ball between the lines until it passes through one line of players, after which all players try to kick the ball into their opponent's goal.) In an Anishinaabe (Algonquin) Traditional Story, aurora borealis are the fires started by earth creator Nanabozho (also known as Nanabush). The lights symbolize Nanabozho's bond with people.

• • •

Famous Canadian *aces* from, respectively, the First and Second World Wars are Billy Bishop, officially credited with seventy-two victories, and Buzz Buerling ("The Falcon of Malta"), who shot down twenty-seven enemy planes in one fourteen-day span.

• • •

Awesome aurora facts

❊ "Aurora borealis" is a Roman and Greek term: Aurora is the Roman dawn goddess; in Greek mythology, Boreas is both the north wind and the god of the north wind.

❊ Aurora borealis is usually between 80 and 120 km high, but displays can reach 1,000 km.

❊ Auroras often look like folding curtains of moving light.

❊ The colours of aurora borealis depend upon the molecules the solar wind collides with: green and yellow=solar wind particles and oxygen; red, violet, blue=solar wind particles and nitrogen.

❊ Aurora borealis has a southern hemisphere twin called "aurora australis," which generally occurs at the same time, with the same shapes and colours.

❊ Aurora borealis makes weird noises like crackles, hisses, and pops.

Anne of Green Gables, the lively, red-haired orphan created by Canada's L. M. Montgomery, has a worldwide following, particularly in Poland, Japan, and Canada. It is thought that more than 50 million copies of the book have been sold. During the Second World War, Montgomery's books were part of the Resistance black market trade in Poland, and they were also issued to Polish soldiers heading to the front. There is an L. M. Montgomery School in Warsaw. *Anne* was added to the Japanese school curriculum in 1952. Japan has national fan clubs, an Anne academy, the Green Gables School of Nursing, and thousands of citizens who flock to Prince Edward Island each year.

Anne of Green Gables–The Musical has a Guinness World Record for the world's longest-running annual musical, and the CBC series *Road to Avonlea*, which is based on the Anne books, is one of the most watched television series in Canada. "Anne of Green Gables" is a registered trademark owned jointly by the heirs of L. M. Montgomery and the Province of Prince Edward Island. For a time in the 1990s, Prince Edward Island licence plates carried the tagline "Home of 'Anne of Green Gables.'" Each year, more than 125,000 people from all over the world visit Green Gables Heritage Place in Prince Edward Island, which has a population of approximately 153,000.

———————— ••• ————————

Canada's *astronauts*[1] have a unique world view:

ROBERTA BONDAR: "Canada needs individuals to whom educators can point, and of whom we can be proud, whether athletes or astronauts or anything else. I think the role each of us plays is not so much 'Look at me,' but rather, 'Look at our country.'"

MARC GARNEAU: "When you go around the planet and look down, you think about the fact that this is the cradle of humanity, that this is a place where 7 billion people, two hundred countries, live side by side, that we share this place and there's nowhere else to go. When you look out and you see that very thin atmosphere—which is like the last layer on the outside of an onion; it's that thin, and it allows life to exist on this planet—the atmosphere, the oceans: these are common things we share, and therefore we have common obligations to take care of them."

CHRIS HADFIELD[2]: "Holding onto the side of a spaceship that's moving around the Earth at 17,500 miles an hour, I could truly see the astonishing beauty of our planet, the infinite textures and colors. On the other side of me, the black velvet bucket of space, brimming with stars. It's vast and overwhelming, this visual immersion, and I could drink it in forever."

JEREMY HANSEN: "You have to get very comfortable with saying, 'Well, every day, I'm just going to give my best. I have skill sets I've learned, I'm going to employ them, and my best is going to be good enough.'"

STEVEN MACLEAN: "You actually saw the Earth breathing: out during the day, and in during the night. If you think about the physics of that, the exchange of the oxygen atoms off the surface of our atmosphere, you realize that it's fragile and we need to look after it."

JULIE PAYETTE: "When I saw the Earth from above, personally, as a spacecraft operator, it certainly reinforced and drove home the fact that there's one place where we can live right now. The 7 billion of us are sharing a wonderful planet, and it's an absolute privilege to see it from above."

DAVID SAINT-JACQUES: "If your dream isn't scary, it's not big enough. Sure, use your head, get a job. But don't lose sight of wonder."

ROBERT THIRSK: "Earth is a tiny, fragile oasis of life, and what's most important is human survival. And you see that so clearly from orbit."

BJARNI TRYGGVASON: "The global warming [problem] is so clear when you look at it from space. A lot of people don't want to accept the fact that this is so. Space is a great vantage point to look back at the Earth and get a far better understanding of the Earth that we're living on and what we're doing to it."

DAFYDD WILLIAMS: "I tell you, looking at the Earth from the end of the Canadarm at that moment, I lived a lifetime."

——————— ••• ———————

Launched in 1972, the *Anik A-1* was the world's first geostationary satellite for domestic communications. Unlike the satellites of other countries, Canada's Anik A-1 had no military function but was instead a telecommunications tool for national unity. Julie-Frances Czapla of St. Leonard, Quebec, won a national "name the satellite contest" in 1969 with her submission of the name "Anik," which means "brother" or "little brother" in Inuktitut. The name was deemed appropriate because it encompasses the ideas of brotherhood and unity that the government wished to foster with the satellite. The decision to allocate millions of dollars to Anik was applauded by those who perceived a benefit to national unity in providing live programming and stable communications to northern Canada. The project was denounced by those who dismissed it as another attempt at assimilation and wondered why the government would allocate so much money to a satellite instead of better housing, improved access to medicine and education, and clean water for Inuit people.

–––––––––––––– ••• ––––––––––––––

The *Acadians* were settlers from France who first set down roots in Nova Scotia, New Brunswick, Prince Edward Island, and Maine during the late sixteenth century. From 1755 to 1763, approximately ten thousand Acadians were deported and had their lands seized by immigrants from New England. Many Acadians eventually relocated to Louisiana, where their Acadian culture evolved into Cajun culture. When they were allowed to return to Canada after 1764, the Acadians settled in New Brunswick, Nova Scotia, and Prince Edward Island.

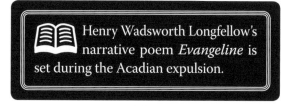

Henry Wadsworth Longfellow's narrative poem *Evangeline* is set during the Acadian expulsion.

–––––––––––––– ••• ––––––––––––––

A Companion of the Order of Canada, *Margaret Atwood* (1939–) is one of Canada's—and the world's—best-known writers. A poet, novelist, literary critic, essayist, inventor, and teacher, she has won numerous national and international awards. Her works have been translated into multiple languages, and many have been adapted for film and television.

In 2017, the television adaptation of *The Handmaid's Tale* won numerous Emmy Awards, including for best drama series. Atwood's 2018 announcement that she was writing a sequel to *The Handmaid's Tale* made global headlines. Prior to its official release on September 10, 2019, *The Testaments* was already in the running for two major literary awards: the Man Booker Prize and the Giller Prize. As soon as the novel hit bookstands, it became a bestseller. As an inventor, Atwood created the LongPen, a remote device that allows an author to sign books from a distance via the Internet. Atwood is also a political and environmental activist. She claims to be a bad typist and a terrible speller. Her office is O. W. Toad (an anagram for *Atwood*).

MARGARET ATWOOD: "Canadians are fond of a good disaster, especially if it has ice, water, or snow in it. You thought the national flag was about a leaf, didn't you? Look harder. It's where someone got axed in the snow."[3]

——————— ••• ———————

Doris Anderson (1921–2007) was an educator, writer, and activist who was made a Companion of the Order of Canada in 2002. Anderson was opposed to the "first past the post" system of electing Canadian governments and advocated strongly for proportional representation. Throughout the latter part of the twentieth century, she was at the forefront of women's issues in Canada. As editor of *Chatelaine*, she doubled its circulation by creating a focus on feminist ideas. She was president of both the National Action Committee on the Status of Women and the Canadian Advisory Council on the Status of Women. Because of Doris Anderson, women's equality rights are part of the Canadian Charter of Rights and Freedoms.

Margaret Atwood's award-winning novels

* *Lady Oracle* (1976)
* *The Handmaid's Tale* (1985)
* *Cat's Eye* (1989)
* *The Robber Bride* (1993)
* *Alias Grace* (1996)
* *The Blind Assassin* (2000)
* *MaddAddam* (2014)
* *The Heart Goes Last* (2016)
* *Angel Catbird, Volume One* (2017)
* *The Testaments* (2019)

B

B IS THE *BLUENOSE*
   THAT'S ETCHED ON THE DIMES
AND SAILED THE ATLANTIC
   IN EARLIER TIMES

BLACK BEARS AND BEAVERS
   IN BANFF NATIONAL PARK,
BETHUNE, BEOTHUK,
   AND BOATS OF BIRCHBARK

The Nova Scotia schooner *Bluenose* gained international fame for fishing and for racing. The record holder for the largest catch of fish hauled into Lunenburg, Nova Scotia, the *Bluenose* dominated the International Fishermen's Trophy races during the 1920s and 1930s. The "Queen of the North Atlantic" appeared at the 1933 Chicago World's Fair and the Silver Jubilee of King George V in 1935.

After being sold to the West Indies Trading Company in 1942, the *Bluenose* sailed the Caribbean, carrying war supplies to the Americans. On one such occasion, when the *Bluenose* was carrying aviation fuel and dynamite, a German U-boat unexpectedly surfaced beside it, but the German captain let it go because he recognized the vessel and he believed it was merely fishing. (Like a great captain before him, Cabot, the *Bluenose* captain was a master of the fish story.) In keeping with a few other Canadian institutions, the *Bluenose* suffered a rather inglorious demise. In 1946 it collided with a reef near Haiti and sank.

The *Bluenose* first appeared on the Canadian dime in 1937 and was inducted into Canada's Sports Hall of Fame in 1955. It was featured on a 37-cent stamp in 1988.

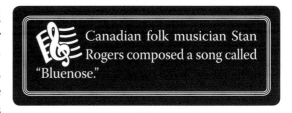
Canadian folk musician Stan Rogers composed a song called "Bluenose."

The *black bear* is the most common bear in Canada. It has been extirpated on Prince Edward Island but lives in every other province and territory in Canada. In the wild, its diet is 95 percent vegetarian and 5 percent insects, mammals, and birds; however, black bears are very happy to reverse those percentages if they have access to human foods and garbage. Bears do not actually hibernate. Instead, after fattening up in the early fall, they go into a lethargic sleep that, depending on climate, lasts from October to May.

The kermode (known as "Spirit Bear") is a black bear with white fur that lives in the Great Bear Rainforest of British Columbia. It is not albino: the white colour is caused by a recessive gene. Traditional Stories of the Gitga'at and Kitasoo peoples explain that after the glaciers receded, Raven (creator of the rainforest) decided to make one out of ten black bears white as a reminder of the white ice and snow.

The *beaver*, an official symbol of Canada, appears on the nickel. It is the largest North American rodent. The beaver has influenced and changed Canada's geography and history more than any other animal. Great loggers and engineers, beavers cut down trees with their ever-growing teeth. They build dams, canals, and lodges. Their dams, which create valuable wetlands, rarely break because the beavers inspect and repair them daily. Their canals, which can be hundreds of metres long, provide an easy way to transport their food (the leaves and bark of trembling aspen, poplar, willow, and birch). Beaver homes are animal palaces with two storeys and in-ground swimming pools. They usually have an above-water feeding den, an above-water resting den, a source of fresh air, and two underwater escape tunnels. During the fall, beavers plaster their lodges with mud to make a solid outer shell that their animal predators cannot penetrate.

The beaver was the basis for the fur trade in Canada during the 1600s and 1700s. Indigenous peoples and the early fur traders used birchbark canoes to transport beaver pelts, which were then shipped overseas for use in the European hat industry. Europeans made beaver hats by felting the soft under-fur of beaver pelt. The beautiful, wide-brimmed, water-resistant hats were such status symbols they were sometimes bequeathed to children in wills. Nearly 6 million beavers were killed in the Canadian fur trade. Luckily, silk hats became fashionable before the beaver went extinct.

Did You Know?

❦ Beaver hats were said to have special powers and were thought to make people smarter, improve memory, and cure deafness.

❦ For ninety years, *Canada's History* was known as *The Beaver*. The magazine, which was started by The Hudson's Bay Company in 1920, had Canada's longest-running brand problem until it finally changed the name in 2010. The name change was partially stimulated by the numerous computer filters that prevented the magazine from showing up on school computers.

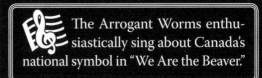
The Arrogant Worms enthusiastically sing about Canada's national symbol in "We Are the Beaver."

From archaeology, we know that the Banff area has been a hot piece of real estate for at least ten thousand years. In 1883, some railway workers came across mineral waters (later called Banff Hot Springs). This led to the establishment of *Banff National Park*, Canada's first national park. Tourists were encouraged to use the hot springs and to get there by railroad.

——————— ••• ———————

The *Beothuk* were the Algonkin-speaking Indigenous people of the island of Newfoundland, and they were the first Indigenous people in Canada to encounter Europeans. The Beothuk painted their bodies and canoes with red ochre, which is possibly why the term "Red Indian" was used to refer to Indigenous people. European contact proved deadly for the Beothuk, and they became extinct in 1829 when Shanawdithit, the last known Beothuk, died.

——————— ••• ———————

Norman Bethune (1890–1939) was a surgeon, an inventor, and an activist. He invented rib shears (still in use today) and other surgical instruments. During the Spanish Civil War, Bethune developed a mobile blood transfusion service for the battlefront. He was an early (and unpopular) proponent of universal health care in Canada. Bethune moved to China, where he is revered for his work as a doctor and as a humanitarian.

Although Bethune was arguably the most world-famous Canadian in the twentieth century (being known to approximately 1 billion Chinese people), he was relatively unknown in Canada until the 1970s. This was because no Canadian government wanted to call attention to a known Communist. In 1970, the Canadian government established diplomatic relations with China, and subsequent Chinese visitors to Canada always asked to visit the Bethune "shrine." Eventually, in response to pressure from the Chinese ambassador, the Canadian government purchased the former Bethune family home in Gravenhurst, Ontario, and converted it into a museum called Bethune Memorial House. The Conservative government of Stephen Harper, eager to do business with China, even added a Visitors' Centre in 2012.

——————— ••• ———————

Traditionally, *birchbark canoes* were the primary means of transportation for many

Indigenous peoples. They favoured birch-bark for several reasons:

* Birch trees are readily available throughout Canada.
* Birchbark is a renewable resource: it is not necessary to kill the tree to harvest the bark.
* Because the bark grows around the trunk of the birch tree, it is easier to harvest and use than the vertical bark from other kinds of trees.
* Birchbark does not shrink, so sheets can be sewn together.
* Birchbark canoes were much better than elm canoes or dugout logs.
* They were lightweight, smooth, waterproof, and strong.
* They could carry heavy loads but could also be carried over portages by one or two men.
* They kept goods and passengers dry.

———————— ••• ————————

C

C IS CANADIAN CONFEDERATION
AND THE CPR'S ROLE IN BUILDING A NATION

CARDINAL, CANADARM,
    CANOE, CIRQUE, AND CARLETON
COUREURS, COFFEE CRISP,
    CBC, COHEN, CLARKSON

Canadian Confederation could be considered the unlikely offspring of a dysfunctional family made up of one aloof patriarch (Great Britain), thirty-six fathers, squabbling siblings (the provinces), and one unruly uncle (Uncle Sam, the United States of America). Throughout the nineteenth century, the Province of Canada struggled as Canada East (Quebec) and Canada West (Ontario) consistently worked against each other. In the meantime, Uncle Sam set the Atlantic provinces economically adrift by unilaterally ending the Reciprocity Treaty. Then, excessively and expressively enthusiastic about expansion, Uncle Sam invented a new concept called "Manifest Destiny," and American citizens started rallying behind such anti-social slogans as "Fifty-four forty or fight!" (J. Polk) and "Speak softly and carry a big stick" (T. Roosevelt). The Fenians didn't talk much about invading Canada; they just went ahead and did it. Great Britain intervened to rid British North America of Washington, Oregon, and one-third of the British Columbia coastline. Canadians began to suspect that neither the British nor the Americans had Canada's best interests at heart.

Motivated largely by fear, greed, and self-interest, the provinces of British North America began to join forces. In 1867, New Brunswick, Nova Scotia, Ontario, and Quebec united. British Columbia joined Confederation in 1871, but only after Canada promised to build a railroad to the west coast. Prince Edward Island joined in 1873 upon the condition that Canada assume its debts and provide a steamship service. Canada purchased Rupert's Land (which the Hudson's Bay Company had stolen from Indigenous peoples) and The Dominion of Canada became a reality—all achieved without involving Indigenous people or women, neither of whom was allowed to vote.

———————— ••• ————————

The *Canadian Pacific Railway Company (CPR)* was incorporated in 1881 with the mandate to build the trans-Canada railway that was a condition of British Columbia's entry into Confederation. British Columbia became a province in 1871, and the last spike of the railway was driven in 1885. The building of the railroad stimulated industrialization and commerce, inspired engineering feats, gave rise to the adoption of standard time, and opened the Canadian West. The railroad made Canada possible, but it was also plagued by scandal—government cash infusions, tax concessions, land grants, rights of way, the monopoly clause, the importation of Chinese labour, and abrogated rights of Indigenous peoples.

———————— ••• ————————

The 1999 recipient of Canada's highest architectural honour, the Gold Medal of the Royal Architectural Institute of Canada, *Douglas Cardinal* (1934–), was booted out of the University of British Columbia in his second year of studies because his designs were unusual and his ancestry was Indigenous. Members of the university's architectural board told Cardinal—who has Siksika (Blackfoot) and German roots—that it took several generations to produce an architect, and that the son of a "half-breed trapper" had little chance of succeeding in the field.[4]

After completing his architectural studies in the United States, Douglas Cardinal moved to Alberta, where he developed a distinctive Indigenous style of architecture. His internationally acclaimed designs are gracious buildings of great beauty and soul that seem to flow out of the landscape as if the earth itself is presenting a gift to humans. His seamless,

A selection of iconic Douglas Cardinal buildings

- ❋ Canadian Museum of History (formerly Canadian Museum of Civilization; Gatineau, Quebec)
- ❋ Cardinal Studio (Stony Plain, Alberta)
- ❋ Gordon Oakes Red Bear Student Centre (Saskatoon, Saskatchewan)
- ❋ National Museum of the American Indian (Washington, DC)
- ❋ St. Albert Place (St. Albert, Alberta)
- ❋ St. Mary's Church (Red Deer, Alberta)
- ❋ Telus World of Science (Edmonton, Alberta)

flowing, curvilinear buildings are made of materials that are evocative of history and landscape and that express the sustainable interweaving of humans and nature. This is not surprising, given the philosophical ideals that underlie all of Cardinal's work: we have an endless capacity to create; we have a responsibility to our gift of creativity; our humanness is the most important aspect of our endeavours; all human efforts should strive for the betterment of all; there is a connectedness between all living things and our environment; our buildings tell stories (of where we come from, who we are, and who we might become).[5]

Douglas Cardinal has received numerous awards, including Officer of the Order of Canada, the Governor General's Award for Visual and Media Arts, the Queen Elizabeth II Diamond Jubilee Medal, and an award from UNESCO for best sustainable village. He was declared a World Master of Contemporary Architecture by the International Association of Architects.

Did You Know?

✤ St. Albert Place was the first building in the world designed by computer. Because of his complex designs, Douglas Cardinal was one of the first architects to use computers. The Canadian government chose his firm as a demonstration site to develop Canadian CAD (computer-assisted design).

✤ In 2015, HuffPost named the Canadian Museum of History one of the ten most beautiful buildings in the world.[6]

Acclaimed actor, director, producer, and writer *Lorne Cardinal* (1964–) was the first Indigenous person to receive a Bachelor of Fine Arts degree at the University of Alberta. A pioneer in the field of Indigenous acting, Lorne Cardinal hopes to inspire Indigenous entertainers to smash the white ceiling in the performing arts. He has worked with various

A selection of Lorne Cardinal's many credits

Television roles:

✤ Little Bad Man in *Big Bear* (1998)

✤ Wade Sinclair in *Renegadepress.com* (2004–08)

✤ Constable Davis Quinton in *Corner Gas* (2004–09)

✤ Principal Storm in *Level Up* (2012–13)

Feature films:

✤ *God's Acre* (2016)

✤ *Never Steady, Never Still* (2017)

✤ *Kayak to Klemtu* (2017; Best Actor, 2018 American Indian Film Festival)

Indigenous performing groups, including Toronto's Native Earth Performing Arts, which aims to present to all Canadians dramas with contemporary and traditional Indigenous themes. Lorne Cardinal's hope is that Indigenous casts and productions with Indigenous themes will attract Indigenous audiences, convert them into regular theatre-goers, and encourage Indigenous people to pursue careers in the performing arts. In addition to acting in and directing theatre productions, Lorne Cardinal produced the documentary *Chasing Lear* (2016).

—————————— ••• ——————————

Tantoo Cardinal (1950–), legendary Indigenous actress and political activist, is renowned not only for her acting ability, but also for her commitment to fighting racial discrimination in the performing arts. She received worldwide recognition for her 1990 performance as Black Shawl in *Dances With Wolves*, a film that sought to correct some of the negative portrayals of Indigenous peoples that had previously characterized American films.

Tantoo Cardinal has accumulated numerous acting awards, including the Earl Grey Award from the Academy of Canadian Cinema and Television and the Technicolor Clyde Gilmour Award from the Toronto Film Critics Association, and she is a member of the Academy of Motion Picture Arts and Sciences in the

A selection of Tantoo Cardinal's credits

Feature films & TV movies:
- *Loyalties* (1986)
- *Candy Mountain* (1987)
- *Divided Loyalties* (1990)
- *Dances With Wolves* (1990)
- *Black Robe* (1991)
- *Legends of the Fall* (1994)
- *Smoke Signals* (1998)

Television series:
- *Spirit Bay* (1982–87)
- *Street Legal* (1987–94)
- *Dr. Quinn, Medicine Woman* (1993–95)
- *North of 60* (1993–97)
- *Moccasin Flats* (2003–06)
- *Mohawk Girls* (2010–17)
- *Blackstone* (2012–15)

United States. She is an active environmentalist and is the recipient of an Eagle Spirit Award from the American Indian Film Festival. In 2006, Tantoo Cardinal was added to the Dreamspeakers Walk of Honour in Edmonton, Alberta, and in 2009 she became a Member of the Order of Canada.

TANTOO CARDINAL: "Things have to change, the truth has to be told, the misrepresentations have to be eliminated."[7]

—————— ••• ——————

The *Canadarm* (a.k.a. the Shuttle Remote Manipulator System) was the Canadian-built remote-controlled mechanical arm that, beginning in 1981, NASA used for three decades in its space shuttle program. The Canadarm was used ninety times before it was retired in 2011. Canadarm2 (a.k.a. the Space Station Remote Manipulator System) was launched in 2001 and used to build the International Space Station. Through the Canadarm, Canada has distinguished itself in the fields of advanced manipulator systems and robotics.

Some free-floating but weighty facts to explain why the Canadarm was out of this world:

* It would have been unable to support its 410 kg weight in Earth's gravity.

* Canadarm could pick up objects that were free-floating in space.

* The original Canadarm could lift more than 30,000 kg on Earth (or up to 266,000 kg in space) at speeds of up to 60 cm/second (depending on payload mass) and accurately place payloads in any position within 5 cm of the target.

* Canadarm could do amazing things in space: build the International Space Station; fix the Hubble Telescope; launch, deploy, and retrieve satellites; monitor the state of each shuttle to ensure protective tiles were intact after arrival in orbit; move astronauts and equipment.

* Canadarm made possible the Canadian Space Agency and gave Canada its astronauts. Impressed by the Canadarm, NASA invited Canada to submit astronaut applications. Canada's first astronaut, Marc Garneau, flew aboard the space shuttle *Challenger* as a payload specialist in 1984. Later, Canadian astronauts trained as mission specialists; Marc Garneau and Chris Hadfield were the first mission specialists.

- Canadarm2 was designed to help berth ships at the International Space Station.
- Canadarm2 could be operated from Earth and move like an inchworm around the space station.
- When the first Canadarm was operational, the two Canadarms could be used together in space—a manoeuvre dubbed the "Canadian handshake."

— ··· —

One upon a time, you couldn't canoodle without a canoe. In the early 1900s, before teenagers could cuddle up in cars or movie theatres, canoodling occurred in canoes. The Peterborough Canoe Company had a special line of "girling" canoes that were fitted with a phonograph and a record compartment. It was expected that young couples would do their courting after they pulled into reeds or an inlet—definitely not while shooting rapids.

Why worry about a wheel when you have already invented a *canoe*? The canoe is a cultural icon in Canada, both for its historical importance to Indigenous peoples and to fur traders, and for its recreational importance today. Historically, Indigenous peoples had many uses for canoes: exploration, fishing, the harvesting of wild rice, hunting, recreation, trade, the transport of freight, as well as for travel and war.

The types of canoes varied depending on the location. In the north, the Inuit used covered canoes (kayaks) for hunting and transporting people and goods. On the Northwest coast, Indigenous peoples made dugout canoes by hollowing out wooden logs. The Haida made exquisite canoes by hollowing out giant red cedars, which they subsequently steamed, shaped, carved, and decorated. Some freight canoes had two or three masts and sails and could hold twenty thousand kilograms of weight. Swift and seaworthy, these dugout canoes were also used for whale hunting and for war (with some holding fifty or sixty warriors). The Coast Salish people also had a long tradition of war canoe racing. The people of the Northeast Woodlands and the Great Lakes area constructed bark canoes from the plentiful local supply of birch and elm trees. The birchbark canoe was more highly prized; elm was often a stopgap material with canoes, quickly made and abandoned at the start of a long portage. The Beothuk in Newfoundland had an unusual bark canoe design with a curved bottom, moss-covered rock ballast, and high peaked bow, stern, and middle sections. The Beothuk used this canoe for the sixty-kilometre paddle across the ocean to Funk Island.

Without the canoe, Canada would not exist. Beginning with Samuel de Champlain and Étienne Brûlé (the first coureur de bois), the canoe was essential to the voyageurs and the fur trade and also to Canada's missionaries and explorers. Some famous names travelled by canoe: Father Jean de Brébeuf, Robert Bylot, Lady Jane Franklin, Simon Fraser, Martin Frobisher, Médard Chouart des Groseilliers, Samuel Hearne, Alexander Mackenzie, Peter Pond, Pierre-Esprit Radisson, Sieur de La Salle, Charlotte Small, David Thompson, Sieur de La Vérendrye.

KANAWA magazine
Paddles Up magazine

Around 1750, the French opened the world's first canoe factory at Trois-Rivières, Quebec. Modern canoes are made of wood, aluminum, fibreglass, Kevlar, or Royalex.

PIERRE ELLIOTT TRUDEAU: "Travel a thousand miles by train and you are a brute; pedal five hundred miles on a bicycle and you remain basically bourgeois; paddle a hundred in a canoe and you are already a child of nature."[8]

❋ *The Canoe* (dir. Goh Iromoto)
❋ *Paddle to the Sea* (dir. William Mason, National Film Board of Canada)
❋ "Mr. Canoehead" (series of skits by comedy troupe The Frantics)
❋ The Paddling Film Festival World Tour has been showcasing paddling films since 2006, screened in various locations throughout the world.

Canadian artists Alex Colville, Frances Anne Hopkins, Arthur Lismer, and Tom Thompson were all inspired by canoes.

• • •

Cirque du Soleil began in Baie-Saint-Paul, Quebec, where a troupe of street performers dreamed of creating a Quebec circus that would traverse the world. Cirque du Soleil mixes street performers with athletes, circus artists, music, dance, and costumes. Most recruits are gymnasts, but other performers include giants, little people, whistlers, contortionists, skateboarders, clowns, dancers, opera singers, acrobats, synchronized swimmers, martial arts experts, jugglers, and pickpockets.[9] Cirque du Soleil now performs on every continent except Antarctica.

• • •

Special status for Quebec; rights of minorities; loyalty to Great Britain; historical settlements of Black Loyalists in Nova Scotia; Montréal as the largest city in Quebec; a conservative-minded population with accents similar to Americans—*Guy Carleton*, first Baron Dorchester (1724–1808), was largely responsible for establishing all these hallmarks of the Canada we know today.

A veteran of the Battle of the Plains of Abraham, Carleton served as the governor of Quebec (1768–78), the governor-in-chief of British North America (1785–95), and the commander-in-chief in New York (1782–83). As the governor of Quebec, he came to understand Quebec society of the time and was sympathetic to the French and conciliatory toward the clergy and the seigneurs. He rejected the anglicization of Quebec and was highly influential in the passage of the 1774 Quebec Act, which supported the Roman Catholic Church, retained the French civil code of law, preserved French customs, postponed the advent of representational government, and laid the groundwork for the "special status" of Quebec society.

Carleton led the preparations for the successful defence of Quebec City during the American invasion led by Montgomery

and Arnold in 1775–76. The Constitution Act of 1791 was passed during his tenure as governor-in-chief of British North America. Carleton opposed the separation of the province of Quebec into Upper and Lower Canada, and he recommended that Montréal be part of Lower Canada. Carleton held the position of commander-in-chief in New York from 1782 to 1783, when the American War of Independence was ending. He oversaw the relocation of troops to England, and he refused to leave New York until the Loyalists (later, under his influence, known as the United Empire Loyalists) were safely relocated, urging both Quebec and Nova Scotia to accept them.

Guy Carlton's influence extended beyond the borders of Canada. His administrative system, which was conciliatory toward the French, became a prototype for "crown colonies" (a type of colonial government that eventually evolved into systems of responsible government and a method for colonized countries to gain independence).

•••

The *coureurs de bois* or "runners of the woods" were independent, unlicensed fur traders who opened up exploration and initiated contact with Indigenous groups during the fur trade era. Many of these French men arrived in New France as part of colonial garrisons or to take up minor civil posts. A few became seigneurial landowners. Some came with explorers such as Samuel de Champlain. Most could not find European wives and were lured by a freer, independent, and profitable life in the wilderness. Many lived with Indigenous peoples—especially the Wendat (Huron) and the Anishinaabe (Algonquin)—learned their languages and customs, and married Indigenous women with whom they had children (subsequently known as Metis). The coureurs de bois excelled at hard work, canoeing, hunting, fishing, snowshoeing, and basic survival. They brought trade and competitive prices to Indigenous peoples. The life was hard and the death rate was high. Their zenith was in the last half of the 1600s, after which they were largely replaced by voyageurs (see p. 167).

———————— ••• ————————

Coffee Crisp is the Canadian chocolate bar which, according to its commercials, "makes a nice light snack." This chocolate bar is a sweet Canadian sensation: it was created in Canada; it is made in Canada; it is sold mainly in Canada. Coffee Crisp has been a top seller in Canada for over seventy-five years, but after only three years in the United States, the bar was pulled from American shelves. Apparently, Americans prefer their coffee ground.

———————— ••• ————————

First established in 1936, the *Canadian Broadcasting Corporation (CBC)* is a Crown corporation that provides national radio and television broadcasting in both official languages and some Indigenous languages. Its programs are for, by, and about Canadians. It attempts to foster a Canadian identity through programs that educate, inform, and entertain.

Canadians hotly debate its value and its funding. Some people support the CBC's efforts to create a strong Canadian identity; others see no need for a strong Canadian identity or, in fact, any Canadian identity at all. Conservative governments typically slash funding to the CBC; Liberal governments typically restore its funding.

———————— ••• ————————

It was never about the awards for the man who gave the world the song "Hallelujah." And yet the music and poetry of *Leonard Cohen* (1934–2016) garnered him an impressive array of awards and honours: Companion of the Order of Canada, the Glenn Gould Prize, a Grammy Lifetime Achievement Award, nine Juno Awards, and many more. He was inducted into the Canadian Music Hall of Fame, the Canadian Songwriters Hall of Fame, the Folk Music Walk of Fame, the Rock and Roll Hall of Fame, and the US Songwriters Hall of Fame.

Cohen published several books of poetry, some of which became national bestsellers. In 1969, he was awarded the Governor General's Award for English language poetry for *Selected Poems 1956–1968*. He declined that award and the honour of being featured on a Canadian stamp, rare during a person's lifetime. (Canada Post released a set of three permanent stamps to commemorate his life and music on September 21, 2019, the eighty-fifth anniversary of his birth.)

In his public appearances Leonard Cohen was gracious, humble, eloquent, and humorous. His gift for delivering memorable lines was displayed in his poetry, in his lyrics, and in his public remarks. While delivering his Canadian Songwriters Hall of Fame acceptance speech, he said: "If I knew where the good songs came from, I'd go there more often."[10]

•••

Canada's 26th governor general, *Adrienne Clarkson* (1939–), was the first refugee, the first member of a visible minority, and the first person of Asian descent to be appointed to the vice-regal position. In spite of the Chinese Immigration Act, which at the time prohibited Chinese immigration

> ## Some Leonard Cohen albums of note
> * *Songs of Leonard Cohen* (1967)
> * *Songs of Love and Hate* (1971)
> * *New Skin for the Old Ceremony* (1974)
> * *Death of a Ladies' Man* (1977)
> * *I'm Your Man* (1988)
> * *The Future* (1992)
> * *You Want It Darker* (2016)

to Canada, Clarkson and her family arrived in Canada with one suitcase apiece not long after the Japanese invaded Hong Kong in 1941.

She was the first non-politician and non-military figure to be appointed governor general. Prior to her investiture, Adrienne Clarkson was a well-known, fluently bilingual Canadian writer, broadcaster, and journalist. During her term (1999–2005), Governor General Clarkson travelled extensively. She continued to promote the arts in Canada, nurtured ties between Canada's northern and southern communities, created the Governor General's Northern Medal (recognizing northern citizens whose work contributes to national identity), and brought a sense of modernity to the vice-regal position. She also raised eyebrows when she remarked that prospective candidates for the position should be required to pass a Canadian knowledge test, and when she stated that the Letters Patent of 1947 transferred final authority of the state from the monarch to the governor general.

Not known for penny-pinching, her administration's budget was cut after a controversial $5 million "northern identity tour" to Finland, Iceland, and Russia in 2003. Since leaving office, Clarkson's extensive use of the expense program for former governors general has prompted members of the press to demand transparency and accountability from Rideau Hall with respect to money matters.

In 2005, Clarkson and her husband, John Ralston Saul, co-founded the Institute for Canadian Citizenship—a charitable organization that helps new citizens integrate into Canadian culture. The year 2009 saw the publication of Clarkson's biography of Norman Bethune and the creation of the Clarkson Cup, the championship trophy for the semi-professional Canadian Women's Hockey League. In late 2011, she published *Room For All of Us: Surprising Stories of Loss and Transformation*, which explores the immigrant experience by profiling ten individuals and their stories. The topic of Clarkson's 2014 CBC Massey Lectures was *Belonging: The Paradox of Citizenship.*

Clarkson is the recipient of numerous honorary doctorates, many broadcasting and television awards, and is a Companion of the Order of Canada.

•••

D

D IS LORD DURHAM
    WHO WANTED ONE NATION
AND ALSO DEMANDED ASSIMILATION

DAWSON, DIONNES, DENE,
    DOGS, DINOSAURS,
DESMOND, DUMONT, DION,
    AND DOUKHOBORS

In his *Report on the Affairs of British North America* (1838), the British politician *Lord Durham* recommended the union of Upper and Lower Canada and the granting of responsible government to British North America. Durham also called for the cultural assimilation of the French, who, he claimed, "had no literature and no history."[11] This did not sit particularly well with French Canadians, who, for a "people without literature," had somehow managed to acquire excellent reading, writing, and translation skills. They objected to English being the sole official language of government; they rejected the idea of French assimilation; and they refused to take responsibility for paying Upper Canada's debts.

Durham's report stimulated French opposition to their imposed minority status and ultimately led to legislative bilingualism in Canada. Many French Canadians have loyally retained their anti-Durham sentiment throughout the centuries. Separatists quoted Durham as a reason to support Quebec separation during the 1995 referendum on Quebec independence.

———————— ••• ————————

George Mercer Dawson (1849–1901) was a Canadian Renaissance man—adventurer, botanist, diplomat, ethnologist, explorer, geographer, geologist, historian, linguist, orator, poet, toponymist, and zoologist. A gentleman and a scholar, he was the inspiration for many place names in Canada, notably *Dawson City* ("the town of the City of Dawson"). Dawson had predicted the presence of gold in the Klondike River a decade before the Klondike Gold Rush. During the Klondike Gold Rush, William Ogilvie agreed to survey the townsite at the confluence of the Klondike and Yukon rivers on the condition that he could name the site after George Dawson, a man he held in very high esteem.

In 1858, *Simon James Dawson* (1820–1902) surveyed the land that ten years later became the *Dawson Trail*—the only all-Canadian route that linked Lake Superior to the Prairies.

Reasons the government wanted to construct the Dawson Trail:

* Canadian passengers would not need to cross international borders. They would not have to deal with the cumbersome paperwork, duties, and taxes that always had to be sorted out between Canada and the United States.

The Dawson Trail

What was advertised: an easy, fast, comfortable journey for valued passengers.

What wasn't advertised: The route from Prince Arthur's Landing (now Thunder Bay) to Fort Garry (now Winnipeg) included lakes, rivers, portages, and jarring rides on corduroy roads built over muskeg. The journey took one month and passengers had to unload and reload their luggage seventy times.

What passengers didn't like:

✱ filthy station houses

✱ leaky, unsafe boats

✱ non-existent meals

✱ sleeping on the ground

✱ destroyed baggage

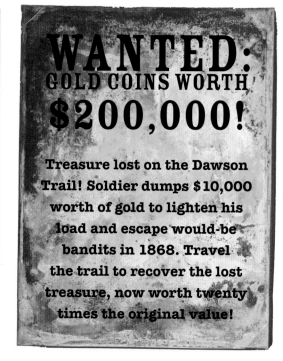

WANTED:
GOLD COINS WORTH
$200,000!

Treasure lost on the Dawson Trail! Soldier dumps $10,000 worth of gold to lighten his load and escape would-be bandits in 1868. Travel the trail to recover the lost treasure, now worth twenty times the original value!

✱ Land-hungry Americans had their eyes on the area, and the Fenians were invading. The Canadian government was afraid the Americans would succeed in seizing Canadian lands. Canada needed to establish a presence in the territory so Americans could not claim the land was unoccupied.

✱ The construction of the Dawson Trail would provide work for western settlers whose crops had failed.

✱ Somebody in an office in Ottawa thought building roads in northern Ontario would be easy.

The difficult task of constructing the Dawson Trail over lakes, rivers, and muskeg was made even more difficult by fires and floods that destroyed large portions of the road as it was being built.

The year before its completion in 1871, General Wolseley and his troops had the misfortune of traversing the Dawson Trail while en route to quell the Red River Resistance. It was apparently not the most pleasant of journeys. Hugh John Macdonald, son of Prime Minister John A. Macdonald and a member of Wolseley's 1870 expedition, wrote that the men "pitched our tents, had supper and went to bed having first cursed old Dawson."[12]

———————— ••• ————————

The *Dionne quintuplets*, five identical girls—Annette, Cecile, Emilie (d. 1954), Marie (d. 1970), and Yvonne (d. 2001)—became a worldwide sensation upon their birth in 1934. The government of Ontario removed them from their parents, and for nine years they were Canada's biggest tourist attraction. People paid to watch them play, putting $500 million into Ontario's coffers. In 1998, the three surviving quintuplets received an apology and a $4 million settlement from the Ontario government for mismanagement of the girls' trust fund.[13]

———————— ••• ————————

The *Dene* is a group of Indigenous peoples whose homeland stretches from Alaska through central and northwestern Canada to the American Southwest. "Dene" is an Athapaskan word for "people." Archaeologists hypothesize that the Dene migrated to Canada by crossing the Bering Strait eight to twelve thousand years ago. Scientists have found genetic, cultural, and linguistic links between the Dene and the Navajo and the Apache.

———————— ••• ————————

The Canadian Kennel Club recognizes four *dog* breeds as uniquely Canadian: Canadian Eskimo dog (also called Canadian Inuit Dog and the Qimmiq), the Labrador retriever, the Newfoundland dog, and the Nova Scotia duck tolling retriever. A fifth indigenous breed, the Tahltan bear dog, was previously recognized but has been declared extinct.

1. CANADIAN ESKIMO DOG

The Qimmiq is the official animal of Nunavut, with roots that possibly go back to 4000 BCE. It is known to have migrated with the Thule people across the Bering Strait between 900 and 1100 CE. Traditionally, the Inuit used this dog for fishing, hunting, protection, and transportation. The dog of superlatives, the Qimmiq could pull the heaviest loads (between 45 and 80 kg), cover the longest distances (24 to 113 km per day), and do so eating the smallest amount of food. Its hunting instincts allowed it to locate seal breathing holes, attack and hold at bay musk ox and polar bear, warn Inuit hunters of cracks in sea ice, and find its way home in blinding snowstorms.

Numbering around twenty thousand in the 1950s, their ranks had dwindled to less than two hundred dogs by the 1970s. The availability of store-bought food, disease, snowmobiles, and the proliferation of settlements (where Qimmiq behaviour deteriorated, causing many to be shot by police) all contributed to their demise. The Eskimo Dog Research Foundation in the Northwest Territories began a breeding program by purchasing specimens from the remnant population of dogs kept by the Inuit of the Boothia Peninsula, Melville Peninsula, and parts of Baffin Island. The numbers are slowly recovering, but the breed is still at risk because of settlements, snowmobiles, and cross-breeding with strays.

Did You Know?

Northern Indigenous peoples traditionally use the dogsled for winter transportation. Drivers of dogsleds are called "mushers" because in Canada's infancy, when French Canadian drivers shouted "marche," English-Canadians misinterpreted the word as "mush."

---

2. LABRADOR RETRIEVER

Very popular as a pet, the Lab is intelligent, affectionate, and obedient. The Labrador descended from dogs taken to Newfoundland by explorers, fishermen, and settlers and evolved by natural selection. They are excellent at retrieving fish and game. Labrador retrievers work as gun dogs, police dogs, as guide dogs for the blind, and as war dogs (trained to serve on battlefields as guards, messengers, scouts, trackers, and in any other capacity).

3. NEWFOUNDLAND DOG

This breed might have descended from the Tibetan mastiff or the Viking "bear dog." An excellent swimmer, the Newfoundland dog is bred for sea work and water rescue. They are gentle, intelligent, loving, and loyal. They are much beloved as family companions and protectors. In nineteenth-century Britain, it was fashionable to own a Newfoundland dog, and many were exported there.

Did You Know?

✻ Sergeant Gander, a Newfoundland dog, was a Canadian Second World War hero in the Battle of Hong Kong. He saved the lives of countless Canadian soldiers. Time and time again, he retrieved live Japanese grenades and threw them over a hill, away from the Canadian soldiers. He died when a grenade exploded between his jaws. He has been honoured with a statue in Gander Heritage Memorial Park in Gander, Newfoundland.

✻ Nana, the nanny in J. M. Barrie's *Peter Pan*, is a Newfoundland dog.

---

4. NOVA SCOTIA DUCK TOLLING RETRIEVER

The Nova Scotia duck tolling retriever, smallest of the retrievers, is an intelligent, affectionate decoy dog who lures ducks to the water's edge by frolicking about on shore chasing sticks and disappearing and reappearing until curious ducks arrive to investigate. A wonderful playmate and family pet, this dog comes with a few warning labels. The American Kennel Club refers to it as a "tornado" and mentions that if you play fetch with a toller until your right arm falls off, he will ask you to throw left-handed. Other breeding sites remark that he might chase your cat, but he rarely means any harm. Every single breeder warns that you should not own this dog if you do not like a high activity level.

···

In Canada, the first recorded *dinosaur* fossils were found by *George Mercer Dawson*, who worked for the Geological Survey of Canada. The Royal Tyrrell Museum in Drumheller, Alberta, has one of Canada's largest dinosaur collections, much of it collected in Dinosaur Provincial Park. These fossils date from the Cretaceous period, which ended about 65 million years ago. At that time, the subtropical landscape was covered with lush forests and huge rivers that flowed into a shallow inland sea. Mud and sand deposits quickly buried and preserved dead dinosaurs. Dinosaur trackways have been found in British Columbia, in northern Alberta, and in Nova Scotia; dinosaur eggs have been found in southern Alberta.

Fossil hotspots

* **British Columbia:** Tumbler Ridge (dinosaur trackways); Yoho National Park (Burgess Shale fossils)

* **Alberta:** Dinosaur Provincial Park (Cretaceous era fossils); Devil's Coulee (dinosaur nesting site); Pipestone Creek (bonebeds)

* **Saskatchewan:** Eastend (Tyrannosaurus rex); East Block, Grasslands National Park (mammal fossils, Cretaceous-Paleogene boundary)

* **Manitoba:** Morden (marine reptile fossils)

* **Ontario:** Rock Glen (Devonian fossils)

* **Quebec:** Miguasha National Park (Devonian fossils)

* **New Brunswick:** Norton (fossil forest)

* **Nova Scotia:** Wasson Bluff (dinosaur trackways); Joggins Fossil Cliffs (carboniferous fossils); Parrsboro (Triassic and Jurassic fossils)

* **Prince Edward Island:** Prince Edward Island National Park (Dimetrodon footprints)

* **Newfoundland:** Mistaken Point (Ediacaran fossils)

* **Northwest Territories:** Hay River area (walking fish tracks)

* **Yukon Territory:** Klondike gold fields (ice-age fossils)

* **Nunavut:** Fossil Creek Trail (Ordovician marine fossils)

Now and again a person appears and reminds us that choices define the individual and that a society is only ever as civilized as the choices it makes. *Viola Desmond* (1914–1965) was one such person. As a young biracial woman, Desmond opted for one of the very few educational career paths open to Black females in post-Depression Nova Scotia. Only a handful of Canadian institutions accepted Black students, so she received her training at Field Beauty Culture School in Montréal before furthering her education in the United States. Upon her return to Halifax, she opened Vi's Studio of Beauty Culture, developed a personal line of beauty products, and started the Desmond School of Beauty Culture, where she trained and mentored Black women from Nova Scotia, New Brunswick, and Quebec. As an independent and successful businesswoman, entrepreneur, and teacher, Viola Desmond earned a position of status and authority in Halifax's Black community.

Almost a decade before American Rosa Parks refused to give up her seat on an Alabama bus, Viola Desmond took a stand against racism by refusing to leave the whites-only section of a theatre in Nova Scotia. On a road trip in 1946, Desmond was detained in New Glasgow because of car trouble. She decided to go to a movie at the Roseland Theatre. Unaware of the theatre's unofficial policy of segregated seating, she requested a ticket for the main floor. Unbeknownst to her, she was given a cheaper ticket for the balcony and was subsequently denied entrance to the main floor. Thinking an error had been made, Desmond returned to the cashier to pay the difference and exchange her ticket, only to be told, "I'm sorry but I'm not permitted to sell downstairs tickets to you people."[14] Desmond opted to take a seat on the main floor anyway.

As a result, Desmond was arrested, injured while being forcibly removed from the theatre, jailed overnight, denied legal representation, fined twenty-six dollars, and convicted of a criminal offence for defrauding the provincial government of the one cent amusement tax (the difference in price between the balcony and main floor tickets) even though she had tried to pay it at the theatre. With monetary assistance from the Nova Scotia Association for the Advancement of Coloured People (NSAACP) and moral support from Carrie Best, founder of *The Clarion*, the province's second Black-owned newspaper, Viola Desmond appealed the judgment in one of the first known legal challenges against racism brought by a Black woman.

Injustice prevailed and Desmond's criminal conviction remained on the books. After her marriage failed, Desmond left for Montréal, and then for New York, where she remained for the rest of her life. Despite her personal losses, Viola Desmond became a rallying point in the fight against racial discrimination in Canada.

On April 15, 2010, Viola Desmond was given a free pardon from the lieutenant-governor of Nova Scotia, The Honorable Mayann Elizabeth Francis (the first Black Nova Scotian to hold that position and the second Black Canadian to hold the position of lieutenant-governor after Ontario's Lincoln Alexander). Premier Darrell Dexter offered an apology and acknowledged that the entire affair had been a miscarriage of justice.

Gabriel Dumont (1837–1906) was a Metis leader who possessed amazing skills as a marksman, hunter, and horseman. Concerned about his people's future as the bison herds decreased and European settlers increased, he led the North-West Resistance of 1885. He was also briefly a member of Buffalo Bill Cody's Wild West Show.

Did You Know?

✻ The image of Viola Desmond graces a 2012 Canadian stamp.

✻ In 2018, Viola Desmond became the first Canadian woman to be featured on the face of a Canadian banknote (the ten dollar bill).

✻ That same year, the Canadian government declared Viola Desmond a National Historic Person.

✻ In February 2019, the Royal Canadian Mint announced the release of its first Black History Month coin, a pure silver coin featuring an engraved portrait of Viola Desmond.

Celine Dion's platinum albums

✻ *Celine Dion* (1996)

✻ *Unison* (1997)

✻ *The Colour of my Love* (1999)

✻ *Let's Talk About Love* (1999)

✻ *Falling Into You* (2001)

✻ *A New Day Has Come* (2003)

✻ *One Heart* (2003)

✻ *All The Way...A Decade of Song* (2005)

✻ *Miracle* (2005)

✻ *These Are Special Times* (2005)

✻ *Taking Chances* (2008)

Celine Dion (1968–), who was born in Charlemagne, Quebec, has sold more albums than any other female musician in music history, has won numerous national and international music awards, and is a Companion of the Order of Canada.

———————— ••• ————————

From 1899 to 1902, around eight thousand *Doukhobors* fled Russia to escape inequality and oppression and to embrace a new life of equality and freedom in Saskatchewan. The Doukhobor mass settlement was one of the largest undertakings in communal living in North America. From the beginning, there were clashes between Doukhobor practices and Canadian institutions. Doukhobor traditions included a belief in equality and a rejection of church liturgy, of secular governments, and of individual ownership of land. The Doukhobors practiced communal living, pacifism, abstinence from alcohol, and vegetarianism. These beliefs and practices were at odds with Canadian culture. In Saskatchewan, the Doukhobors could register for individual homesteads, but they were not allowed to live communally. After the Doukhobors refused to swear an oath of allegiance, the Saskatchewan authorities cancelled their homestead titles, and most Doukhobors moved to British Columbia, where their radical pacifism was not always well received by that provincial government.

During both world wars, the Doukhobors were disenfranchised because of their pacifism. During the 1950s and 1960s, the radical sect called Sons of Freedom, unhappy with government intrusion in their lives, protested with arson, bombings, and nudity (the last to demonstrate spiritual freedom from material possessions). These actions resulted in approximately two hundred Doukhobor children being taken from their parents and placed in a special school.

In 2004, the BC government issued to the Doukhobors a statement of regret. Today, descendants of the original Doukhobor settlers number around twenty-five thousand, with approximately one third of that number participating to various degrees in Doukhobor culture.

E

E IS EXPLORERS
    WHO WENT ON A QUEST
TO SCOUT OUT THE LAND
    FROM THE EAST TO THE WEST

ELECTRIC CAR HEATERS
    AND EH? AND EGG CARTONS,
EXPO AND EASY-OFF
    AND ALSO POOR EATON'S

Eh?

Canada's *explorers* are innovators, facilitators, and survivors who make and document new discoveries, introduce new ways of thinking, and establish new fields of inquiry and enterprise.

The first explorers of the land now known as Canada were Indigenous peoples. Through investigation, they established a vast knowledge base and developed innovative technologies that allowed people not only to survive but to thrive in Canada's harsh environment and climate. As they explored, Indigenous people created trails, found portage sites, named places, learned about the medicinal properties and nutritional benefits of plants, and developed survival strategies for a harsh environment. They created technologies that are still used in modern times: canoes, dogsleds, kayaks, many different types of shelters, snowshoes, and toboggans.

Indigenous peoples were also facilitators, guides, and rescuers for the European explorers whose enthusiasm exceeded expertise. Because Indigenous peoples assisted European explorers, the fur trade was established in Canada.

THANADELTHUR's diplomatic, linguistic, and scouting skills enabled the Hudson

* Keskarrah and Green Stockings guided Sir John Franklin.
* Matonabbe guided Samuel Hearne.
* Nika guided René-Robert Cavelier, Sieur de La Salle.
* Otchaga guided Pierre Gaultier de Varennes, Sieur de La Vérendrye.
* Eenoolooapik guided William Penny.
* Tookoolito and Ebierbing guided Charles Francis Hall.

Bay Company to establish a trading post at Churchill. Without Indigenous peoples, it is unlikely that early European explorers could have survived winters in Canada. Sometimes, Indigenous peoples had to rescue Europeans. When several members of Hall's northern expedition were marooned on an ice floe, their guides TOOKOOLITO and EBIERBING kept them alive for six months.

SAMUEL DE CHAMPLAIN (ca. 1567–1635) is called the "Father of New France." His discoveries on behalf of France led to the strong French influence in Canada.

SIR ALEXANDER MACKENZIE (ca. 1764–1820) was the first European explorer to cross the North American continent.

DAVID THOMPSON (1770–1857), who was accompanied on his travels by his wife, Charlotte Small, possessed an amazing sense of curiosity as well as extraordinary map-making skills.

JOSEPH BURR TYRRELL (1858–1957) discovered the area that is now Dinosaur Provincial Park. The first to find an Albertosaurus, he initiated paleontology in Canada.

VILHJÁLMUR STEFANSSON (1879–1962) located the Copper Inuit people. He started modern anthropology in Canada by being the first explorer to use the techniques of participant observation and ethnography to study the Inuit and the Arctic.

CATHERINE PARR TRAILL (1802–1899) was one of the first Canadian botanists; her works document the natural history of nineteenth-century Canada.

PHYLLIS MUNDAY (1894–1990) and DON MUNDAY (1890–1950) spent decades in the twentieth century exploring and mapping the Coast Range of British Columbia.

Canadian paleontologists, anthropologists, archaeologists, geologists, and astronauts continue to make discoveries. Canadian explorers today also investigate the oceans and other aspects of geography such as extreme weather. To name just two, Jill Heinerth explores underwater caves and icebergs, and Greg Johnson explores severe weather and is a storm-chaser.

———————— ••• ————————

Electric car heaters, *egg cartons*, and *Easy-Off* are Canadian inventions. In 1892 Thomas Ahearn patented the electric car heater, replacing the need for lap robes and rugs, heater boxes, and gas heating lamps. After hearing an argument about broken eggs between a hotelier and a deliveryman, newspaper publisher Joseph Coyle invented the egg carton; patented in 1918, it made millions—but not for the inventor. Herbert McCool of Regina invented Easy-Off Oven Cleaner in 1932; he originally sold it door to door.

———————— ••• ————————

ACROSS

1. The "Father of New France" founded a colony in 1603 and lived there until 1635.

6. In the 1570s this pirate searched for the Northwest Passage and found fool's gold.

7. In 1754 and 1759, he paddled with Cree guides up the Saskatchewan River to the Battle River Valley.

10. He told fish stories after visiting the Grand Banks in 1497.

13. In 1925, this husband and wife mountaineering team found Mt. Waddington, the highest peak in BC, and in 1928, they climbed it.

14. From 1857 to 1860, he explored a triangular area in the southern prairies that he claimed was ill-suited for civilization.

15. Henry Hudson's mate, he explored the eastern Arctic between 1611 and 1616.

16. He traded furs in the Athabasca area in the late 1770s.

DOWN

1. He explored and mapped the St. Lawrence River from 1534 to 1542.

2. He inspired the Lewis and Clark expedition by being the first European to cross North America, reaching the Arctic Ocean in 1789 and the Pacific in 1793.

3. Around 1000 CE, he explored the east coast of North America and found wild grapes.

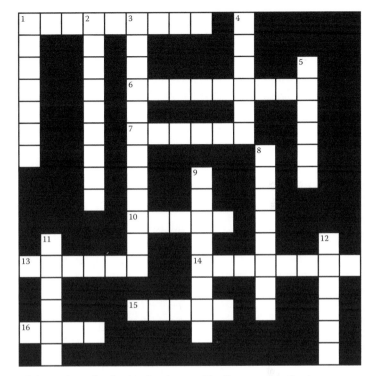

4. While working for the Hudson's Bay Company between 1690 and 1692, he was the first European to see the Prairies.

5. In 1808 this fur trader explored the river that bears his name.

8. This explorer and his crew disappeared in the Arctic in 1845.

9. In the 27 years he spent mapping Canada (1784–1811), he covered more than 80,000 km by foot and by canoe.

11. He disappeared after he was set adrift in James Bay during a mutiny on his ship in 1611.

12. The first European to cross the Arctic by land, he witnessed the Massacre at Bloody Falls in 1771.

Explorers to choose from: *Bylot; Cabot; Cartier; Champlain; Franklin; Fraser; Frobisher; Hearne; Henday; Hudson; Kelsey; Leif the Lucky; Mackenzie; Munday; Palliser; Pond; Thompson* (Answers on p. 46)

CROSSWORD PUZZLE ANSWERS

ACROSS
1. Champlain
6. Frobisher
7. Henday
10. Cabot
13. Munday
14. Palliser
15. Bylot
16. Pond

DOWN
1. Cartier
2. Mackenzie
3. Leif the Lucky
4. Kelsey
5. Fraser
8. Franklin
9. Thompson
11. Hudson
12. Hearne

Although many Canadians deny that they ever say "*eh*," this interjection is included as a Canadianism in many dictionaries. Linguist Elaine Gold, founder of the Canadian Language Museum, has identified ten ways in which Canadians use "eh":[15]

1. Statement of opinion (Nice day, eh?)
2. Statement of fact (It goes over here, eh?)
3. Commands (Think about it, eh?)
4. Exclamations (What a game, eh?)
5. Questions (What are they trying to do, eh?)
6. To mean "pardon" (Eh? What did you say?)
7. In fixed expressions (Thanks, eh?)
8. Insults (You're a real snob, eh?)
9. Accusations (You took the last piece, eh?)
10. Telling a story/the narrative eh (This guy is up on the twenty-seventh floor, eh? Then he gets out on the ledge, eh?)

Quite a piece of work, eh?

——————— ••• ———————

Expo 67 was the climax of Canada's Centennial celebrations. Without so much as a wink at the women's liberation movement, the theme of the World's Fair in Montréal was "Man and his World."

——————— ••• ———————

The T. Eaton Company Limited was a major Canadian department store that operated throughout North America for more than one hundred years. It was famous for its innovative practices (cash sales, fixed prices, and refunds for dissatisfied customers) and for its mail-order catalogue. Prior to the 1884 introduction of the *Eaton's* catalogue, rural pioneers had to trade their excess produce for the limited goods available in local general stores. The Eaton's catalogue suddenly made available a huge variety of goods that could not be purchased locally. In the west, the Eaton's catalogue was often called "the homesteader's bible." A huge hit with rural Canadians, the catalogue was despised by small-town shopkeepers because they could not compete with the variety, the prices, or the money-back guarantees. Sometimes, sympathetic postmasters would throw out the catalogues instead of delivering them. By the early 1900s, Eaton's and its catalogue were Canadian institutions. Founded in 1869, the company went bankrupt in 1999.

Did You Know?

Eaton's was an important part of Christmas for millions of Canadians because of the Santa Claus Parade and the Christmas Catalogue. Even reluctant readers couldn't wait to read the Eaton's Christmas Catalogue because it contained an extensive, not-too-expensive toy section.

The first Eaton's Santa Claus Parades were held in Toronto and Winnipeg in 1905, and in Montréal the parade ran from 1925 to 1968. Eaton's Santa Claus Parade was the longest parade in North America (often 2.4 kilometres in length), and it covered a 6-kilometre route. Eaton's Santa liked to vary his mode of transportation and at different times throughout the years turned up in a sleigh pulled by four live reindeer from Labrador, a train, an airplane, a chariot, and even on a silver fish. From the 1950s onward, the event was televised across Canada and in the United States. The last Eaton's Santa Claus Parade was in 1982.

F

F IS THE FLAG, THE RED MAPLE LEAF,
A SYMBOL OF UNITY,
TOLERANCE, PEACE

FIRST NATIONS, FIDDLEHEADS,
FIERCE FENIAN RAIDS,
THE FAMOUS FIVE, FOX,
FONYO, FUR TRADE

The Maple Leaf (l'Unifolié) became Canada's *flag* when it was unfurled on Parliament Hill on February 15, 1965. It is one of the very few world flags that features an aspect of living nature—the leaf of the maple tree. The white square in the middle is called a Canadian pale.

Prior to the Maple Leaf, Canada used first the Union Jack and later the Red Ensign. In the 1960s, the ruling Liberal Party wanted a distinctive Canadian flag to help unify the country and to promote a sense of nationalism, but many others (the opposition Conservative Party of John Diefenbaker, and some legionnaires, veterans, journalists, and Canadians of British descent) were opposed to it because they thought it would mean that Canada was severing ties with Britain. The Great Flag Debate was one of the most bitter fights ever fought in the House of Commons. Even after the matter went to a parliamentary committee, the debate raged on. Prime Minister Lester B. Pearson finally invoked closure and the matter was settled in December 1964.

Vexillologists (those who study the history, symbolism, and usage of flags) consider Canada's Maple Leaf flag to be extremely successful.

Vexillologist Report

Country: Canada
Flag: Maple Leaf

❋ Striking   A+
❋ Simple   A+
❋ Recognizable   A+

• • •

First Nations is a broad term for Indigenous peoples in Canada who are not Metis or Inuit. They are the descendants of the first inhabitants of the land now known as Canada. There are more than six hundred First Nations communities in Canada. First Nations people reject the Doctrine of Discovery and *terre nullius.* (By international law, if a European nation "discovered" non-European lands, the European nation gained the land title and had sovereignty over the "discovered" lands, regardless of who lived there at the time of "discovery." It is based on the premise that a land is unoccupied if no Christians are living there.) First Nations people declare themselves sovereign nations, and they claim the right to self-determination (to practice their own political, legal, economic, social, and cultural systems).

The grassroots "Idle No More" movement began in 2012 to protest the Harper Government's infamous Bill C-45, which infringes upon First Nations sovereignty and environmental protections. Started by four Saskatchewan women (Jessica Gordon, Sylvia McAdam, Sheelah McLean, and Nina Wilson), Idle No More has become one of the largest First Nations mass movements ever and it "calls on all people to join in a peaceful revolution, to honour Indigenous sovereignty, and to protect the land and water."[16]

———————— ••• ————————

The *fiddlehead*, or ostrich fern, is a native plant found mainly in Ontario, Quebec, and New Brunswick. The coiled end can be cooked and is a good source of vitamins A and C. A traditional Indigenous food, the fiddlehead today is a springtime delicacy that is served in fancy restaurants. Harvesters of fiddleheads are not just fiddling around: the New Brunswick fiddlehead industry earns millions of dollars each year.

———————— ••• ————————

The *Fenian raids* occurred from 1866 to 1871. A secret society of Irish patriots who had emigrated to the United States decided it would be a good idea to take over Canada and then trade it back to Britain in exchange for Irish independence. Canada was less than happy to be considered ransom, and Britain was not amused. The raids were not successful, but they did lead to loss of life. The benefit to Canada was a strengthened military and greatly increased support for Confederation.

———————— ••• ————————

The Famous Five was a group of five Alberta women (Henrietta Muir Edwards, Nellie McClung, Louise Crummy McKinney, Emily Murphy, and Irene Parlby) who participated in the famous "Persons Case" that went to the Privy Council of Britain in 1929. They successfully argued that women were "persons" under the British North America Act and could therefore be appointed as judges and to seats in the Senate. They won a tremendous victory for women's rights in Canada. The unanimous decision stated: "The exclusion of women from all public offices is a relic of days more barbarous than ours. And to those who would ask why the word 'person' should include females, the obvious answer is, why should it not?"[17]

runner who touched the world in 1980 with his Marathon of Hope. At the time, Fox planned to run across Canada to heighten the awareness of cancer and to raise funds for cancer research. He ran from St. John's, Newfoundland, to Thunder Bay, Ontario, where he was forced to stop when he developed lung cancer. He died less than a year later, at the age of twenty-two. The Terry Fox Foundation, which organizes the annual Terry Fox Run that takes place in communities across the country, has raised hundreds of millions of dollars for cancer research.

--- ••• ---

Did You Know?

Some of the many other Canadians who have fought for human rights in Canada:

✻ **Black rights:** Mary Shadd Cary, Viola Desmond
✻ **Indigenous rights:** Mary Two-Axe Earley, Ga'axstal'as (Jane Constance Cook), Nahnebahwequay (Catherine Sutton), Viola Robinson
✻ **LGBTQ rights:** Jeremy Dias, Jim Egan, Gloria Eshkibok, Richard Fung, Jack Nesbit, Nancy Nicol, Svend Robinson, Douglas Stewart
✻ **Women's rights:** Thérèse Casgrain, Marie Lacoste Gérin-Lajoie, Lise Payette, Bertha Wilson
✻ **Workers' rights:** Hannah Gale, Agnes Macphail, Madeleine Parent, Eileen Tallman Sufrin

--- ••• ---

Inspired by Terry Fox, *Steve Fonyo* (1965–), another one-legged runner, ran across Canada in a "Journey for Lives." Fonyo dipped his prosthesis in the Atlantic Ocean in March 1984 and repeated the action in the Pacific Ocean in May 1985. Steve Fonyo also raised millions of dollars for cancer research. A controversial Canadian hero, Fonyo was awarded the Order of Canada, only to have it revoked in 2009 because of his criminal record.

--- ••• ---

The youngest-ever recipient of the Companion of the Order of Canada (Canada's highest civilian honour) was *Terry Fox* (1958–1981), the one-legged

For approximately 250 years, the *fur trade* was Canada's largest commercial undertaking. The first fur traders were whalers and fishermen off the Grand Banks (see p. 55). In the early 1600s, during the weeks fishermen spent onshore drying their fish, they traded cloth and metal goods for fresh meat and furs from Indigenous peoples. The fishermen found a ready market in Europe for the furs, which were primarily beaver. Beaver felt hats became fashionable in Europe, and the demand for furs increased. French traders arrived in Canada and set up bases in Acadia and Quebec. As the number of fur traders increased, profits decreased, until the French government began to issue monopolies to certain traders who were expected to support French land claims and to help convert Indigenous peoples to Christianity. Cardinal Richelieu established the Compagnie des Cent-Associés (Company of One Hundred Associates), which, supported by profits from the fur trade, sent out Catholic missionaries (including the Jesuits) and settlers.

As time went on, more settlers arrived, many of whom became coureurs de bois. Faced with a shortage of European women in the settlements and a need to master Indigenous survival skills, the coureurs de bois formed close kinship ties with Indigenous peoples by marrying Indigenous women. Their offspring subsequently formed a new Indigenous group— the Metis.

In 1670, the English awarded themselves one-third of the land that is now Canada, formed the Hudson's Bay Company (HBC), set up trading posts near Hudson Bay, and waited for Indigenous peoples to arrive with furs. French voyageurs undercut the HBC by travelling to the Indigenous communities and trading with them there.

More settlers and explorers arrived and moved westward. The HBC was forced to expand westward, building forts that have since become western cities. The HBC faced competition from the North West Company, which allowed all employees to take Indigenous wives, thus expanding kinship ties with Indigenous groups and increasing the Metis population. Missionaries, adventurers, government expeditions, and scientists followed the fur traders into the interior of the country.

As the fur trade continued, more lands and control were acquired by Europeans. Indigenous peoples became more dependent on European goods, suffered huge population decreases due to European diseases, and lost their lifestyle and control of their lands. They have had to fight ever since for their sense of identity and their human rights. The European takeover of the land was fairly peaceful due to the fur trade, which began as a partnership between Europeans and First Nations, and because of the intermarriages during the fur trade. The spirit of cooperation in order to survive that has characterized Canadian society has its roots in the fur trade; however, many of the problems faced by Indigenous communities today stem from European actions during the fur trade. The near extinction of the beavers during the fur trade also presaged many environmental problems that did not exist prior to European arrival in what is now Canada.

———————— ••• ————————

G

G IS GREY OWL,
    WHO PREACHED CONSERVATION
BUT PROVED TO BE ENGLISH,
    TO OUR CONSTERNATION

GRAND BANKS AND GREAT LAKES,
    THE GREY CUP, THE GRIZZLY,
G-SUITS AND GOALIE MASKS,
    GREENPEACE AND GST

A scandal arose after the death of *Grey Owl* (1888–1938), a Canadian who preached conservation during the 1920s and 1930s, when it turned out that instead of being an Indigenous person he was actually an Englishman of questionable morals. His real name was Archibald Stansfeld Belaney. Enthralled with the idea of the "noble savage," he dyed his hair and skin to look like an Indigenous person's, spent years learning Indigenous customs, and claimed to be the offspring of a Scottish father and an Apache mother. He lived in the Canadian wilderness, making a living as a trapper and a guide.

After he met his fourth wife, a Kanienkehaka (Mohawk) woman whom he called Anahareo, he gave up trapping and turned his attention to conservation. He became a naturalist with Riding Mountain National Park and Prince Albert National Park. He is credited with saving the beaver from extinction. His three bestselling books, his educational films, and his lecture tours in England, Canada, and the United States made him famous and focused international attention on conservation. In his heyday, Grey Owl filled lecture halls, became one of Canada's best-known writers, sat for celebrity photographer Yousuf Karsh, dined with the prime minister, and was granted an audience with the royal family of Great Britain.

———————— ••• ————————

The *Grand Banks* are a series of underwater plateaus off the southeast coast of Newfoundland. The mix of the cold Labrador Current and the warm Gulf Stream in the shallow water lifts nutrients from the extensive animal and plant life at the bottom to the surface. Historically, these nutrient-rich waters were full of fish, particularly cod. Viking explorers and then Portuguese and Basque fishermen were probably the first Europeans to fish off the Grand Banks.

After his voyage in 1497, John Cabot reported that the fish in the Grand Banks were so numerous they were blocking the boats. A true master of the fish tale, Cabot claimed that his crew used the backs of cod as stepping stones to walk across the waters and that his men merely dipped baskets into the water to fill them with fish. Cabot's reports attracted fishermen from England, France, Portugal, and Spain, and later from other countries as well.

For more than four hundred years, Newfoundland's economy was based on fishing off the Grand Banks. Overfishing finally caused the collapse of the cod stocks, and, in 1992, the Canadian government imposed a moratorium on the commercial fishing of cod. Now home to the Hibernia oil field, the area is also known for heavy fog and icebergs.

• • •

The *Great Lakes* (Superior, Huron, Michigan, Erie, Ontario) hold approximately one-fifth of the world's surface supply of fresh water. Lake Michigan is entirely in the United States; the other lakes border Canada and the United States. The largest island in the Great Lakes is Manitoulin and the last shipwreck was the *Edmund Fitzgerald* in Lake Superior in 1975.

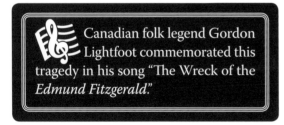
Canadian folk legend Gordon Lightfoot commemorated this tragedy in his song "The Wreck of the *Edmund Fitzgerald*."

• • •

The *Grey Cup* refers to both the Canadian Football League (CFL) championship event and the trophy that is awarded to the winning team of the Grey Cup game. The Grey Cup was first donated by Governor General Earl Grey in 1909 (predating the American Super Bowl's Vince Lombardi Trophy by more than a half century).

The Grey Cup festival owes its origins to the Calgary Stampeders and their fans, who rode the rails to Toronto for the 1948 Grey Cup game. Cowboys, chuckwagons, and a hotel-loving horse celebrated all week long with parties and pancake breakfasts at City Hall. Modern-day festivities include parties, luncheons, performances on outdoor stages, and all sorts of food. The climax is, of course, the Grey Cup game.

Since 1962, the Grey Cup game has been televised to all Canadians because the Canadian government considers it an important instrument of national unity. It is the most highly rated television program in Canada.

• • •

The ferocious *grizzly bear* lives primarily on plant life in British Columbia, Alberta, and the Yukon, Northwest, and Nunavut territories. Grizzlies have been extirpated on the Prairies, and the remaining western

The remarkable (mis)adventures of Canada's Grey Cup

* **1909:** Governor General Earl Grey decides he'd like to donate a trophy for Canadian amateur men's hockey, but Sir Montagu Allan beats him to it. The Grey Cup then becomes the trophy for the Canadian football championship.

* **1909:** The first Grey Cup is not awarded to the University of Toronto Varsity Blues champions because Lord Grey forgot to have it made. In the years following, the U of T team might fumble the football, but they stick like burrs to the trophy, refusing to hand it over to subsequent winners until 1914.

* **1947:** The Grey Cup survives a fire at the Toronto Argonauts rowing clubhouse.

* **1969:** The Grey Cup is stolen from a display case and held for ransom. The kidnappers' demands are ignored, because CFL officials say they'll just replace it (after all, the original price tag was $48.00). The kidnappers relent and the cup is recovered at the Royal York Hotel by the Metro Toronto Police, who crown themselves champions by taping "Metro Police ETF" to the trophy. (ETF stands for "Emergency Task Force"—a tactical unit trained to deal with high-risk emergency situations such as terrorist kidnappings and hostage-takings.)

* **1978:** The Edmonton Eskimos break the cup by dropping it.

* **1987:** The Edmonton Eskimos break the cup by sitting on it.

* **1993:** The Edmonton Eskimos break the cup by giving it a head-butt.

* **1996:** The BC Lions break the cup; the base separates from the cup while in their possession.

* **2008:** The Grey Cup travels to Kandahar Air Field in Afghanistan, and personnel pass it around on Canada Day without breaking it.

* **2012:** The Toronto Argonauts break a handle off during celebrations.

* **2014:** The Calgary Stampeders break the cup while handing it around.

* **2019:** The triumphant Blue Bombers return to Winnipeg with the cup in two pieces.

Alberta population is listed as threatened. In British Columbia, they are a species of "special concern" due to degradation or loss of habitat, accidental deaths on roads and railways, and low reproductive rates. Grizzlies rarely attack humans. If a grizzly does make contact with a human, the human should "play dead" (hard to do if one's heart is racing).

———————— ••• ————————

The *G-suits* worn by astronauts today are derived from the pressure suit invented by Canadian Wilbur Rounding Franks. A graduate of the University of Toronto medical school, Franks was a colleague of Frederick Banting, who was working on aviation medicine during the early years of the Second World War. After Banting's death in 1941, Franks continued Banting's research into the problem of Allied pilots fainting during high-velocity manoeuvres because gravitational forces prevented adequate blood flow to their brains. Franks designed a suit with a water-filled outer layer that pressed on the legs and abdomen. This pressure prevented blood from pooling lower in the body and allowed free circulation to the brain. (Later designs used air pressure and an inflatable bladder.) The "Franks Flying Suit" was first used in combat in 1942.

———————— ••• ————————

The first hockey net-keeper to wear a *goalie mask* was Elizabeth Graham in 1927. Graham played goal for the Queen's University Golden Gaels women's hockey team and donned a metal fencing mask to protect her dental work. In 1930, Clint Benedict of the Montréal Maroons was the first NHL goalie to wear a mask (a leather nose-guard) to protect a broken nose.

Bill Burchmore invented the fibre-glass face mask that Jacques Plante wore on November 1, 1959, after acquiring a nasty gash in a game against the New York Rangers. From the mid-1950s, Jacques Plante had been experimenting with mask-making and had begun to wear a mask in practices. In 1959, Plante became the first NHL goalie to regularly wear a goalie mask in games. That decision raised questions about his commitment and his bravery; however, his long winning streak with the mask eventually silenced his critics. Plante established a company called Fibrosport and continued to design and produce goalie masks.

———————— ••• ————————

> *When the last tree is cut, the last river poisoned, and the last fish dead, we will discover that we can't eat money...* [18]
> —Proverb on a Greenpeace poster

Now a worldwide environmental organization based in Amsterdam, *Greenpeace* was started in Vancouver in 1971 by a group concerned about nuclear testing in the Pacific. The organization named its flagship the *Rainbow Warrior* after the "Rainbow Prophecy." The prophecy speaks of a time of awakening, when the Warriors of the Rainbow (the keepers of the lore and wisdom) will unite all people to restore love, health, unity, and justice to the earth.

———————— ••• ————————

The *GST* is Canada's unpopular Goods and Services Tax. Endlessly confusing to children and tourists, it is not usually included in the price on the price tag but is added on afterwards at the till.

Initially, the Senate refused to pass the GST. Finally, Progressive Conservative Prime Minister Brian Mulroney, with the approval of Queen Elizabeth II, invoked Section 26 of the 1867 Constitution Act.

This action allowed him to stack the Senate with eight additional Conservatives, giving him the majority he needed to pass the legislation.

The Progressive Conservatives lost the next election to Jean Chrétien and the Liberal Party, who had repeatedly promised to "axe the tax." Once elected, Prime Minister Chrétien kept the tax, although he apologized for "giving the impression" that he would drop it.

———————— ••• ————————

H IS ICE HOCKEY,
   A GREAT SOURCE OF PRIDE,
SUMMER AND WINTER
   IT'S PLAYED NATIONWIDE

HUDSON BAY, HOODOOS,
   HALIFAX EXPLOSION,
HANLAN AND HENDERSON,
   HOWE AND RICK HANSEN

Hockey (a.k.a. ice hockey) is Canada's official national winter sport. It is played year-round on the ice, roads, in alleys, in garages, in halls, in gymnasiums, in basements, and on tables (table hockey being a Canadian invention). It is an unusual sport because its playing field is surrounded by boards, its players wear skates, and play occurs behind the net.

For centuries, games similar to ice hockey (notably field hurley and bandy) were played in Europe; on the North American continent, the Mi'kmaq had long played a type of stick-and-ball game called oochamkunutk, using curved sticks and a wooden puck. In the winter, oochamkunutk players wore skates made from animal jawbones and played the game on ice. Around 1800, students at King's College in Windsor, Nova Scotia, began playing hurley on ice. The Mi'kmaq called this new game alchamadyk, and they also began playing it, mostly against military teams and, later on, college teams.

As the game evolved, so too did the equipment. Highly skilled Mi'kmaw craftsmen carved superior hockey sticks from the roots of hornbeam and birch trees. In 1860, ice hockey players began to use a wooden puck made from cherry wood because it was dark (and thus easily seen on ice) and durable. The cherry wood puck, used until the advent of the rubber puck in 1886, was a Mi'kmaw innovation that military teams adopted after observing that it worked better on ice than the unmanageable hurley ball; use of the wooden puck quickly spread to other teams. John Forbes and Thomas Bateman invented the Acme Club spring skate in 1863 for the Starr Manufacturing Company in Dartmouth, Nova Scotia.

In 1875, a group of McGill University students in Montréal played the first public indoor exhibition game of hockey. It was organized by James Creighton, who brought from Nova Scotia Mi'kmaw sticks, Starr skates, and Halifax rules. There were nine players a side. To reduce the chance of injuries from a ball flying around indoors, they used a flat, circular piece of wood for a puck.

As hockey developed, the rules changed. Teams had seven players (the seventh being a rover) and the defencemen were called the point and the cover-point. The goalie had to remain on his feet at all times, and no forward passes were allowed in the game. An illegal forward pass was called an offside pass.

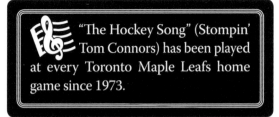

"The Hockey Song" (Stompin' Tom Connors) has been played at every Toronto Maple Leafs home game since 1973.

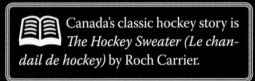

Canada's classic hockey story is *The Hockey Sweater (Le chandail de hockey)* by Roch Carrier.

In 1893, Governor General Lord Stanley donated the first Stanley Cup for the amateur hockey champions of Canada. The Coloured Hockey League of the Maritimes formed in 1895 in response to racial segregation policies that prohibited Blacks and whites from playing on the same teams or in the same league. The National Hockey League was established in Montréal in 1917, and in the 1920s, the Stanley Cup became the property of the league. Since 1952, Saturday night has been *Hockey Night in Canada* on the CBC network.

The first recorded women's hockey games were in Ottawa (1889) and Barrie (1892), Ontario. Women's hockey grew until the Second World War, when it diminished substantially. Society was more conservative after the war, and hockey was not deemed an appropriate activity for females. Today, in Canada, hockey is once again popular with women. Since 1990, the Canadian national women's team has won numerous gold medals at world championships and at the Olympics. From 2009 until the organization's demise in 2019, the Clarkson Cup (named for former Governor General Adrienne Clarkson) was the championship trophy for the Canadian Women's Hockey League.

Marie-Philip Poulin scored the gold-medal winning goals for Canada in two Olympic Games—2010 (Vancouver) and 2014 (Sochi)—and she was captain of the silver-medal team at the 2018 Olympic Games in Pyeongchang. Canadian Hayley Wickenheiser is the all-time leader for goals, assists, and points in Olympic women's ice hockey. While playing for HC Halamat in Finland, she became the first woman to score a goal while playing in a professional men's league.

••••

Hudson Bay in northern Canada was named for Henry Hudson, the first known

European to sail into the bay (before his crew mutinied and left him stranded there). Originally, the name was "Hudson's Bay," but the possessive form was dropped in accordance with rules set out by the Geographic Board of Canada in 1900. By coastline, Hudson Bay is the world's largest bay; by area, it is second in size only to the Bay of Bengal.

Did You Know?

Step on land in Churchill and you are in Manitoba; step into the water at Churchill and you are in Nunavut.

Hoodoos are the strange capped rock formations found in Alberta's badlands. They are the result of weathering and erosion. According to Blackfoot and Cree Traditional Stories, hoodoos are giant petrified protectors that come alive at night to throw rocks at trespassers.

— ••• —

Before the atomic bombs of 1945, the *Halifax Explosion* of 1917 was the largest human-made explosion the world had ever witnessed. The *Imo* (a Belgian relief ship) and the *Mont-Blanc* (a French munitions ship) collided in the Halifax Harbour. A large part of Halifax was destroyed from the resulting blast and tsunami.

Halifax Explosion aftermath

- 2,000 dead; 9,000 injured
- 691 injured by window glass; 41 totally blinded
- 1,630 homes destroyed
- 12,000 homes damaged
- 6,000 without shelter
- +2.5 square kilometres of North End Halifax & First Nations community of Turtle Grove flattened
- $35 million total property damage
- + $20 million in assistance

Did You Know?

- Every year on December 6 the City of Halifax hosts a memorial service at Fort Needham Memorial Park to commemorate the Halifax Explosion. Three levels of government participate in this event, which includes speeches, a recognition of survivors, the laying of wreaths, a moment of silence at 9:04:35 A.M. (the precise time of the explosion), a closing prayer, and the ringing out of the Halifax Explosion Memorial Bell Tower's carillon bells.

❀ Every year, Halifax sends a Christmas tree to Boston—an annual thank you for Boston's assistance. The American city sent doctors, money, and supplies immediately following the 1917 explosion.

———— ••• ————

Ned Hanlan (1855–1908) of Toronto was Canada's first world sporting champion. He was the world's single-sculls rowing champion from 1880 to 1884.

———— ••• ————

Paul Henderson (1943–) scored one of the most famous goals in Canadian hockey history when he put the puck past Soviet goaltender Vladislav Tretiak in the last minute of the last game of the 1972 Summit Series between Canada and Russia. The goal gave Canada the series victory—a feat that was celebrated across the country.

———— ••• ————

Superstar *Gordie Howe* (1928–2016), number 9 for the Detroit Red Wings, winner of numerous awards and four Stanley Cups, is known as "Mr. Hockey." A player has a "Gordie Howe hat trick" if, in one game, he or she scores a goal, gets an assist, and participates in a fight.

———— ••• ————

Rick Hansen (1957–) is the beloved world-class wheelchair track and field athlete who is most well known for his 1987 Man in Motion tour, during which he wheeled himself forty thousand kilometres over twenty-six months, visiting thirty-four countries to raise awareness of and funds for spinal cord research and quality of life initiatives. A celebrated Paralympian and philanthropist, he was made a Companion of the Order of Canada in 1987.

———— ••• ————

I

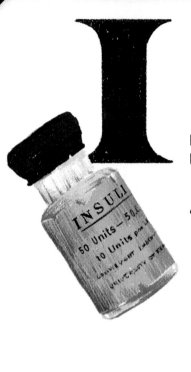

I IS THE INUIT WHO HAVE THE KNACK
FOR BUILDING ICE IGLOOS,
   INUKSUK, INUNNGUAQ

"IN FLANDERS FIELDS," IMMIGRANTS,
   IMAX, INVENTIONS
INSULIN, INK,
   INSTANT REPLAY CONVENTIONS

The *Inuit* (which in Inuktitut means "the people") live primarily in northern Canada. The Inuit are descendants of the Thule people who originated in Asia, crossed the Bering Strait to Alaska, and, around 1300 CE, spread east across the Arctic as far as Greenland. The Inuit are therefore not an isolated cultural group in Canada but rather are part of a large, circumpolar civilization. Their arrival in what is now Canada's Arctic coincided with the disappearance of the walrus-hunting Dorset people (known to the Inuit as Tuniit). The reasons for the demise of the Dorset are uncertain, but it is clear that the Inuit had the advantage of superior technology—better housing, better weapons (sinew-backed bows and throwing harpoons), bigger boats (kayaks and umiaks), metal tools, and the ability to hunt whales.

Initially, there was limited contact between the Inuit and Europeans, but from the nineteenth century onwards, more whalers, fur traders, explorers, missionaries, and government officials made their way to the Canadian north. Interaction with Europeans had a huge impact on the Inuit way of life. Trade increased, and Inuit people became hunters, guides, and interpreters for Europeans. Negative changes included exposure to European diseases, the fluctuation of fur prices, wildlife shortages, residential schools, the loss of nomadic lifestyles, the establishment of permanent settlements, forced relocations, cultural deprivation, the loss of autonomy, and the loss of personal identity during the three-decades-long "identification disk system." This was a system in which each Inuit received a leather, coin-sized disk stamped with a government-assigned

Inuit inventions

* bow drill
* igloo (see p. 69)
* kamiik (boots)
* kayak (see p. 86)
* parka
* qamutiik (sled)
* qulliq (seal-oil lamp)
* snow goggle
* snowshoe
* toggling harpoon head
* ulu (women's knife)
* umiak (see p. 159)

number, which was to be sewn into a parka or worn around the neck at all times. This number replaced the name of the person. Sometimes government officials wrote letters that addressed individuals by disk numbers only and not by personal names.

Here's a timeline of some of the significant twentieth-century changes to Inuit life:

* 1970: Project Surname was established to assign surnames and to replace the disk system.
* 1971: The Inuit Tapirisat of Canada (ITC) was formed to promote land claims in the Northwest Territories.
* 1975: The James Bay and Northern Quebec Agreement established Inuit land ownership and some other rights in Northern Quebec.
* 1984: The Inuvialuit Final Agreement provided the Inuit with a settlement region in the western part of the Northwest Territories.
* 1993: Canada settled an Inuit land claim by awarding the Inuit $1.1 billion and 1.9 square kilometres of land and water (including mineral rights to 35,257 square kilometres within the Inuit portion of land).
* 1999: Nunavut (1.9 million square kilometres of land and water) was proclaimed the third Canadian territory, an act that provided the Inuit with land and also some degree of self-government.

With the establishment of Nunavut, the Inuit have reclaimed the history and geography of their traditional lands. Some geographical sites are now called by their original Inuit names: Frobisher Bay, for instance, has again become Iqaluit, which means "fishes." Nunavut, which has four official languages (Inuktitut, Inuinnaqtun, English, French), has revived a sense of pride in Inuit cultural traditions: Inuit cultural material is included in school curricula; the Inuit Language Protection Act helps preserve Inuit culture and language; and people's names are being re-spelled so that they represent authentic Inuit sounds. There is also renewed interest in Inuit Qaujimajatuqangit (Traditional Knowledge, including storytelling) and in vocal games, drum dancing, and traditional sports and games, which develop agility, balance, endurance, and strength.

* Susan Aglukark
* Tanya Tagaq
* Nukariik (Karin and Kathy Kettler)
* Charlie Panigoniak

* *Angry Inuit* (Alethea Arnaquq-Baril, National Film Board of Canada)
* *Atanarjuat: The Fast Runner* (Zacharias Kunuk)
* *Between Two Worlds* (Barry Greenwald, National Film Board of Canada)
* *The Necessities of Life* (Benoît Pilon)

The traditional winter homes of the Inuit are called *igloos*. The dome-shaped structures are made with blocks of snow placed in a circular pattern. The walls slope inwards to form a self-supporting arch. The ice and snow act as insulators, protecting the inhabitants from the cold and the wind.

Did You Know?

* Igloos are built from the inside.
* On average, the inside of the igloo is 65 degrees warmer than the outside air with wind chill. The Inuit often spread animal skins on the walls, which helps trap heat and prevent melting. Oil lamps also add heat.
* If you have an igloo, you don't need a hill to go tobogganing. Just do like Inuit children: climb onto the roof and slide down the sides.

An *inuksuk* is a stone marker that is a helper to the Inuit. Inuksuit (more than one inuksuk) are used mainly for navigation and hunting. An *inunnguaq* is an inuksuk made into the shape of a human. Once built, inuksuit are considered sacred and it is bad luck to disassemble or destroy them.

———————— ••• ————————

John McCrae (1872–1918), a Canadian surgeon and a lieutenant-colonel, wrote *In Flanders Fields* during the First World War. It is one of the most famous war poems of all time and is recited in many places throughout the world on Remembrance Day. The poem inspired the use of the scarlet poppy as a symbol of remembrance.

———————— ••• ————————

Archaeological evidence suggests that between 16,000 BCE and 1,000 CE, people migrated across Beringia and settled in the lands that are currently known as North, Central, and South America. These people are therefore the Indigenous peoples of Canada.

Immigration to what is now called Canada began around 1,000 CE with the arrival of the Vikings and has continued to the present day with *immigrants* from all over the globe. People have come to Canada as adventurers, business recruits, economic refugees, educators, entrepreneurs, explorers, extended family members, fur traders, inventors, missionaries, political refugees, religious refugees, remittance men (often ne'er-do-well Englishmen who were a source of embarrassment to their families and who were paid to live far away in Canada), scientists, and as indentured labour and slaves. Although some have faced hardships due to climate, cultural differences, language difficulties, poverty, and racism, many immigrants share hope for a better life in Canada and all have enriched Canadian society by sharing their cultures, their talents, and their values.

———————— ••• ————————

Abbreviated Canadian Immigration Timeline

———————— ••• ————————

1000 CE: Leif the Lucky and fellow Vikings settle in Vinland for about a decade.

1598-1603: The fur trade begins and the French attempt to set up colonies.

1598-1853: The fur trade is the largest and most significant commercial enterprise in Canada, involving Indigenous peoples and European colonists who come mainly from England and France to settle in Canada.

1600S: Settlement of French, English, and Blacks.

1604: Samuel de Champlain and his interpreter, Mathieu da Costa (a free Black man), arrive.

1605: Champlain establishes the Habitation settlement at Port Royal in Acadia.

1608-1629: Champlain establishes the first permanent Canadian colony at Quebec.

1610: John Guy establishes the first British colony at Cuper's Cove in Newfoundland.

1628: Six-year-old Olivier Le Jeune is the first Black slave brought directly from Africa to Canada.

1700S: Settlement of English, French, Blacks, Jews, Quakers, United Empire Loyalists, Mennonites, and Maroons.

1701-1775: English and French colonists and Black slaves arrive.

1760: Jewish recruits arrive in Montréal with General Jefferey Amherst.

1770S: Quakers come.

1776: United Empire Loyalists (British, free Blacks, Germans) go mainly to Nova Scotia; Mennonites go to Upper Canada.

1796: Jamaican Maroons arrive in Halifax.

1800S: Settlement of Scots, American Blacks, Irish, British children, Chinese, Jews, Japanese, Doukhobors, and others.

1802: Scottish highlanders arrive in Nova Scotia.

1815-1865: Tens of thousands of American Black refugees arrive via the Underground Railroad.

1845-1850: Three hundred thousand Irish immigrate to urban centres.

1850S & 1860S: Young British girls aged fourteen and up arrive as domestic servants, mainly for farms.

1858: Chinese, Chileans, and Hawaiians come during the Fraser River Gold Rush.

1869-1939: Approximately one hundred thousand British Home Children (aged three to fourteen years) arrive as indentured labour for farms.

1870-1914: Jewish refugees come from Europe.

1877-1928: Japanese settle in British Columbia.

1880S: Mormons settle in southern Alberta.

1881-1885: At least fifteen thousand Chinese railroad workers are recruited to build the CPR.

1895-1905: Americans, French, Germans, Hungarians, Icelanders, Romanians, Scandinavians, and Ukrainians immigrate as farmers to western Canada.

1899: Doukhobors arrive in Saskatchewan.

1900S: Settlement of British, Americans, Europeans, Scandinavians, Jews, Asians, and other visible minorities.

1900-1914: To settle the west, Clifford Sifton (Minister of the Interior, 1896–1905) recruits, in declining order of preference, British, American, French, Belgian, Dutch, Scandinavian, Swiss, Finnish, Russian, Austro-Hungarian, German, Ukrainian, Polish, Italian, South Slavic, Greek, Syrian, Jewish, Asian, Romani, and Black farmers.

1918: Hutterites and Mennonites arrive.

1950S: Ceylonese, Hungarians, Indians, and Pakistanis immigrate.

1960S: Indians, Japanese, and West Indians come.

1970S: Chilean, Khmer, Laotian, and Vietnamese refugees immigrate, as do South Asians expelled from East Africa.

1980S: Vietnamese and Sri Lankan refugees immigrate.

1990S: Bhutanese, Iraqi, Kosovar, Syrian, and Tamil refugees arrive.

2000-2019: Settlement of immigrants from across the globe, primarily Afghanistan, Algeria, Australia, Bangladesh, Brazil, China, Colombia, Democratic Republic of Congo, Egypt, Ethiopia, Federal Republic of Cameroon, France, Germany, Haiti, India, Iran, Iraq, Ireland, Israel, Ivory Coast, Jamaica, Jordan, Lebanon, Mexico, Morocco, Nepal, Nigeria, Pakistan, Philippines, Romania, Russia, Somalia, South Korea, Sri Lanka, Syria, Tunisia, Ukraine, United Kingdom, United States, and Vietnam.

2015-PRESENT: Refugees of the Syrian civil war are welcomed to Canada.

Did You Know?

✹ In 1914, the *Komagata Maru* sailed into Vancouver Harbour carrying four hundred East Indians and was quickly escorted back out again by the brand new Canadian navy, to the accompaniment of cheering and waving Vancouverites on the shore.

✹ The MS *St. Louis* arrived off Nova Scotia in 1939, but the 907 Jewish refugees aboard were denied entry to Canada, and 254 of its passengers later perished in the Holocaust.

• • •

There is nothing small about *IMAX*—including its beginnings, its growth, and its success. IMAX (from "image maximum") emerged as part of the cultural heritage of Expo 67, where its co-founders (Graeme Ferguson, Robert Kerr, Roman Kroitor, and William Shaw) had experimented with new film formats. They

A motley mix of multicultural milestones

❋ **1833:** abolition of slavery in the British Empire.

❋ **1885–1923:** Chinese Head Tax (starting at $50, it rose to $500).

❋ **1911:** "continuous passage" law and immigration tax of $200 for Indians coming from Asia.

❋ **1933–1945:** fewer than 5,000 Jewish refugees from Europe permitted to enter Canada.

❋ **1939–1945:** Japanese Canadians dispossessed and interned; Canadians of German, Italian, and Jewish ancestry relocated; Canadians of Bulgarian, German, Ukrainian, and Turkish origin interned; restricted immigration for Blacks, Germans, Indians, Italians, Japanese, Jews, and Romas.

❋ **1945:** 4,000 Japanese Canadians deported.

❋ **1947:** Chinese immigration banned altogether.

❋ **1960:** Canadian Bill of Rights is the first federal law to protect human rights and freedoms.

❋ **1962:** "whites only" immigration policy scrapped.

❋ **1964–1970:** Africville (Halifax's historic Black settlement) destroyed by order of the city council.

❋ **1967:** new points system introduced for immigration with no quotas or restrictions on the number of potential immigrants.

❋ **1971:** official policies of bilingualism (English and French) and multiculturalism (whereby Canada would formally respect the cultures, languages, and religions of all Canadians) introduced by the government of Prime Minister Pierre Elliott Trudeau.

❋ **1982:** Canadian *Charter of Rights and Freedoms* becomes part of Canada's Constitution and guarantees the same rights and freedoms for all Canadians.

developed the IMAX system, which enlarges film projection while maintaining high-resolution images. The projections (using 70 mm film stock turned on its side) produce images approximately ten times the size of regular film projections. The first IMAX film, *Tiger Child,* made its debut at the 1970 World's Fair in Osaka, Japan. The next year, the first permanent IMAX film theatre opened at Toronto's Ontario Place. Since then, IMAX theatres and films have been showcased at numerous international expositions. More than 1,500 IMAX theatres have sprouted in eighty countries throughout the world; the IMAX film catalogue has expanded to include both documentaries and Hollywood blockbusters; and IMAX has won several national and international film awards. In 1994, IMAX Corporation was sold to American WGIM Acquisition Corporation.

Notable IMAX films
* *North of Superior* (1971)
* *The Dream is Alive* (1985)
* *Fires of Kuwait* (1993)

Two *inventions* that have a Canadian connection are the green *ink* used on American dollar bills and the zipper. The green, counterfeit-proof ink used on American "greenbacks" was invented in Canada by American-born chemist and mineralogist Thomas Sterry Hunt, who worked for McGill University and the Geological Survey of Canada. Gideon Sundback, a Swedish immigrant first to Canada and then to the United States (though he professed that his heart remained in Canada), is credited with inventing the modern zipper (called a "Hookless Fastener") in 1913 while working for the Universal Fastener Company in New Jersey. He later perfected the design and patented the "Separable Fastener" in 1917. He did some of the preliminary work on the Separable Fastener in St. Catharines, Ontario. After moving his household to Pennsylvania, Sundback located his Lightning Fastener Company in St. Catharines. This Canadian company subsequently produced Sundback's zippers.

Canadians have obtained patents for more than 1 million inventions.

INVENTION	INVENTOR	DATE OF INVENTION / PATENT (P)
5-pin bowling	Thomas F. Ryan	1908 or 1909
A.M. radio	Reginald Fessenden	1906
basketball	James Naismith	1891
Bloody Caesar (cocktail)	Walter Chell	1969
butter tarts	Les filles du roi	1663–1673
Canada Dry ginger ale	John J. McLaughlin	1907 (P)
cardiac pacemaker	John A. Hopps	1950
caulking gun (puttying tool)	Theodore Witte	1894 (P)
Coffee Crisp	Rowntree Company	1939
Crispy Crunch	Harold Oswin	1930
Easy-Off	Herbert McCool	1932 or 1933
egg carton	Joseph Coyle	1911; 1918 (P)
electric car heater	Thomas Ahearn	1890 or 1891; 1892 (P)
electric light bulb	Henry Woodward	1874; sold patent to T. Edison
electric wheelchair	George Klein	1953
foghorn (steam)	Robert Foulis	1853
G-suit	Wilbur Rounding Franks	1941
goalie mask (fibreglass)	Bill Burchmore	1959
IMAX	Graeme Ferguson; Robert Kerr; Roman Kroitor; William Shaw	1967
instant mashed potatoes (dehydrated potato flakes)	Edward Asselbergs	1966 (P)
instant replay	George Retzlaff	1955
insulin	Frederick Banting; Charles Best; James Collip; J. J. R. Macleod	1921–1922
Java computer language	James A. Gosling	1994
Jolly Jumper	Susan Olivia Poole	1910
kerosene	Abraham Gesner	1846; 1854 (P)

INVENTION	INVENTOR	DATE OF INVENTION / PATENT (P)
McIntosh apple	John McIntosh	1811
music synthesizer (Electronic Sackbut)	Hugh Le Caine	1945–1948
newsprint	Charles Fenerty	circa 1838
submarine telegraph cable (first in North America)	Fredrick Newton Gisborne	1852
Pablum	Alan Brown; Theodore Drake; Frederick Tisdall	1930
pager	Alfred J. Gross	1949
paint roller	Norman Breakey	circa 1940
peanut butter	Marcellus Gilmore Edson	1884 (P)
photodegradable plastics	James Guillet	1970 or 1971
plastic garbage bag	Larry Hansen; Frank Plomp; Henry Wasylyk (all independently)	circa 1950
Plexiglas	William Chalmers	1930 or 1931
prosthetic hand	Helmut Lucas	1971
quartz clock	Warren Marrison (with American J. W. Horton)	1927
railway sleeper car	Samuel Sharp	1857
Robertson screw	Peter L. Robertson	1907 or 1908
rotary snowplow	J. W. Elliott	1869
snow blower	Arthur Sicard	1925
Superman	Joe Shuster (with American writer Jerry Siegel)	1938
table hockey	Donald Munro; Ralph Grieve	1932; 1934 (P)
telephone	Alexander Graham Bell	1876 (P)
Tilley hat	Alex Tilley	1980
Trivial Pursuit	Scott Abbott; Chris Haney	1979
walkie-talkie	Donald L. Hings	1937
Wonderbra	Louise Poirier	1964; 1971 (P)
Yukon Gold potato	Garnet Johnston	1966

Diabetes has always plagued humans. Ancient Egyptian manuscripts at least three thousand years old contain remedies for "urine which is too plentiful." Ancient Hindus described "honey urine," which attracted flies and ants. Galen, a student of Greek physician Hippocrates, called it "diarrhea of the urine" and "the thirsty disease." Galen's contemporary, Aretaeus, wrote: "Diabetes is a wonderful affection, not very frequent among men, being a melting down of the flesh and the limbs into urine."[19]

For millennia, a diagnosis of diabetes was a death sentence. In the nineteenth and early twentieth centuries, the standard treatment for diabetics was to eat little and prepare to die. Many researchers tried without success to find a cure. In 1921, working under the supervision of J. J. R. Macleod, Frederick Banting and Charles Best succeeded in isolating and extracting a protein hormone in pancreatic islets—a hormone they called "*insulin*"—which they proved could treat diabetes. Biochemist James Collip then helped purify insulin for clinical use.

Did You Know?

In the 1920s, diabetic children were placed in large hospital wards to die while their grieving families watched helplessly. There were sometimes fifty or more children in a ward. One morning in 1922, Banting, Best, and Collip went from bed to bed on a children's ward, injecting each dying child with insulin. As they started injecting the last children, the first ones to be injected began to emerge from comas. For the first time in history, parents watched joyfully as their diabetic children were miraculously snatched back from certain death.

Frederick Banting sold his patent for insulin to the University of Toronto for one dollar, claiming that insulin was for the world, not for him.

The Nobel Prize for Medicine was awarded to Banting and Macleod in 1923. Banting shared his prize and credit with Best; Macleod did the same with Collip. They didn't necessarily always like each other, but the world is indebted to all of them. Frederick Banting was given a knighthood in 1934.

In 1955, George Retzlaff (1922–2003), the producer/director of *Hockey Night in Canada* on the CBC network, invented *instant replay*. He developed a "hot processor" method to make a film recording of a goal. Initially, it took thirty minutes to develop the film, which was then played during intermissions. However, it did gain *instant* popularity.

Hockey Night in Canada highlights

Hockey Night in Canada (*HNC*) is Canada's longest-running television programme and holds the Guinness World Record for longest-running television sports programme. The show has won 22 Gemini Awards and 3 Canadian Screen Awards.

HNC got its name from Foster Hewitt in 1936, when the newly-established CBC took over the *Imperial Esso Hockey Broadcast* on Saturday nights. It wasn't until the 1968/69 season that NHL games were televised in their entirety. Prior to that, the televised games started midway through the second period. This was done to ensure that televised broadcasts did not cause a decrease in ticket sales to the home games—one of the main objections to television broadcasts raised by NHL president Clarence Campbell.

- first radio broadcast (Montréal and Toronto): November 12, 1931 (General Motors Hockey Broadcast; play-by-play: Foster Hewitt)
- first French television airing (Montréal, Montréal Forum): October 11, 1952 (*Hockey Night in Canada*); Montréal Canadiens vs. Detroit Red Wings; play by play: René Lecavalier)
- first English television airing (Toronto, Maple Leaf Gardens): November 1, 1952 (*Hockey Night in Canada*); Toronto Maple Leafs vs. Boston Bruins; play by play: Foster Hewitt)
- 1957: first Canada-wide broadcasts
- 1965: first televised game in colour (March 24; Toronto vs. Montréal)

J IS THE FIRST OF JULY
    CELEBRATION
WHEN PEOPLE REJOICE
    IN CONFEDERATION

JE ME SOUVIENS,
    JOHNSON, JASPER, AND JAVA,
JUNIPER, JADE,
    JOLLY JUMPER, AND JALNA

July 1 used to be called Dominion Day, but in 1982 the name was changed to Canada Day. Today, Canadians celebrate across the country with a variety of free activities and fireworks, but this was not always the case. The first country-wide celebration did not occur until 1967.

July 1 also marks these significant events in Canada:

* 1927: The Canadian National Railway provides Canada's first national radio hookup.
* 1958: The CBC's first cross-country broadcast.
* 1966: Canada's first colour television transmission.
* 1967: The launching of the Order of Canada.
* 1980: The naming of "O Canada" as Canada's official national anthem.

--- ••• ---

Je me souviens (I remember) is the motto of the province of Quebec. It was placed above the main door of the facade of the Hôtel du Parlement in 1883 and has been part of Quebec's coat of arms since 1939.

In 1978, the provincial government realized the phrase would make a good tagline and added it to Quebec license plates.

--- ••• ---

Emily Pauline Johnson (1861–1913), also known as Tekahionwake ("Double Wampum"), was of mixed European and Kanienkehaka (Mohawk) heritage. She was a well-known entertainer in North America in the late nineteenth century, portraying Indigenous culture through cultural artifacts, poetry, other writings, and live dramatic performances. At the height of her popularity, Johnson entertained both as a Kanienkehaka (Mohawk) warrior and as an English lady, often starting a performance in traditional Kanienkehaka dress and then finishing in Victorian garb.

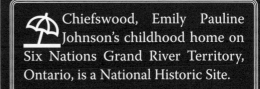
Chiefswood, Emily Pauline Johnson's childhood home on Six Nations Grand River Territory, Ontario, is a National Historic Site.

--- ••• ---

The municipality of *Jasper* is located in Jasper National Park, a UNESCO World Heritage Site in Alberta's Rocky Mountains. The municipality of Jasper was first established in 1813 by *Jasper Hawes* as a fur-trading post for the North West Company. *Jasper National Park* is the largest Rocky Mountain park in Canada, and the world's second largest Dark Sky Preserve.

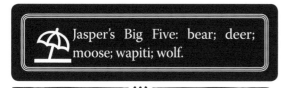

Jasper's Big Five: bear; deer; moose; wapiti; wolf.

Canadian James Gosling (1955–) is considered the creator of *Java*, a computer programming language that he and his team developed for Sun Microsystems in 1991. Java is considered platform-independent because it can run on any operating system. The original mantra for Java was "write once, run anywhere."

Four species of *juniper*, a coniferous evergreen, are native to Canada. Juniper berries are used as a flavouring in gin.

Indigenous peoples used the wood of the Rocky Mountain juniper to make weapons, spoons, and carvings. Sometimes they boiled the boughs to make disinfectants, while the berries were made into medicinal teas.

The world's largest deposits of nephrite *jade* come from British Columbia. The finest jade is called Polar Jade and is used to make jewelry and ornaments.

In 1910, Susan Olivia Poole (1889–1975), a Native American who immigrated to Canada, invented the *Jolly Jumper*. She based her idea on the Indigenous practice of strapping babies into cradle boards and then suspending them from tree limbs. Mothers would pull on the tree limbs to rock the babies. Poole began producing Jolly Jumpers for her grandchildren in 1948, but the product was not patented until 1957.

Mazo de la Roche (1879–1961) wrote the *Jalna* series of novels about an upper-class British family (the Whiteoaks) living on a country estate (Jalna) in a British colony (Ontario). The first of the series, *Jalna*, was published in 1927 to great critical acclaim and was considered by many to be a significant contribution to serious world literature. As the series progressed, the books lost favour with literary critics, who then derided them as soap opera drivel, characterised by melodramatic plots, uninteresting characters, and an outdated loyalist conservatism that celebrated a hierarchical class society and colonial ties to Britain. De la Roche's readers disagreed with the critics, and the series remained popular for many years (both in Canada and abroad) and the books have been translated into several languages.

K

K IS FOR KANATA,
    WHICH IN WENDAT MEANS SETTLEMENT,
JACQUES CARTIER DECIDED
    THE NAME WAS JUST EXCELLENT

KARSH, KAIN, THE KLONDIKE,
    AND ALSO THE KAYAK,
KURELEK, KANE,
    KAKABEKA, KUSUGAK

Most Canadians accept that the name Canada comes from the Huron-Wendat word *kanata*, which means a collection of huts or a community. The sons of Haudenosaunee (Iroquoian) Chief Donnacona referred to the St. Lawrence River as the "chemin de kanata"—the route to the village. Cartier misheard it as "Canada." And the rest is history.

Or maybe not.

Another story holds that early Spanish explorers, having searched unsuccessfully for gold and other riches, declared the Baie des Chaleurs area "aca nada" or "cà nada" (terms that mean "nothing here"). By the time the French explorers arrived, the locals had had enough of Europeans and, hoping to encourage an early departure, repeated the phrase "aca nada." The French, however, thought it sounded like a good name for a country and decided to stay. And the rest is history.

Or maybe not.

The most refreshing account, courtesy of a writer in the 1811 *Kingston Gazette*, is that the country's name finds its origins with the first inhabitants of New France, who thirsted for a "can-a-day" of spruce beer.

We can drink to that.

—— ••• ——

Yousuf Karsh (1908–2002) was a world-renowned Canadian photographer whose portraits of famous people include Lord and Lady Bessborough, Robert Borden, Winston Churchill, Bill and Hillary Clinton, Albert Einstein, Grey Owl, Ernest Hemingway, John F. Kennedy, Martin Luther King, and William Lyon Mackenzie King.

—— ••• ——

In 1973, *Karen Kain* (1951–), a principal dancer with the National Ballet of Canada, won world recognition dancing with her partner, Frank Augustyn, in the renowned Moscow International Ballet Competition. In Canada, Kain and Augustyn were known as ballet's "gold-dust twins," and they came under the mentorship of the Soviet ballet great, Rudolf Nureyev. Following her 1997 retirement from dancing, Karen Kain became artistic director of the National Ballet of Canada.

—— ••• ——

The *Klondike* is a town, a river, and a range of hills in the Yukon. "Klondike" comes from a Gwich'in word, "thron-duik,"

Did You Know?

Sam Steele commanded the Yukon detachment of the Northwest Mounted Police during the Klondike Gold Rush. Steele made himself popular with some by introducing new rules that prevented starvation and the spread of typhoid. Under his leadership, newly arriving miners had to bring adequate food provisions, and Dawson City had to undergo a massive cleanup. Steele made himself unpopular with others when he curtailed corruption by transferring to the police the power to issue mining licenses and to collect royalties.

meaning "hammer river" (so-called because Indigenous peoples used to drive spikes into the riverbed to trap migrating salmon). The area around Dawson City was the site of the Klondike Gold Rush.

— • • • —

Traditionally made of driftwood covered with caribou or seal skins, the *kayak* is a fast, seaworthy, covered-deck Inuit boat. The Inuit wore parkas, which they tied around the rims of the hatch-holes. This made the kayak completely watertight, even if it tipped. For more than two thousand years, the Inuit have used the kayak to hunt, travel, and transport goods. Today, many Canadian communities use kayaks for recreation.

— • • • —

William Kurelek (1927–1977) was an important painter from the Canadian west who was strongly influenced by his prairie roots. Many of his paintings are accompanied by a simple text. Two of his books for children—*A Prairie Boy's Winter* (1973) and *A Prairie Boy's Summer* (1975)—are considered modern Canadian classics.

— • • • —

Paul Kane (1810–1871) was an artist and explorer of the Canadian northwest. From 1846 to 1848, he accompanied the fur-trading canoe fleet of the Hudson's Bay Company from Fort William, Ontario, to Fort Garry, Manitoba, where he observed the last great bison hunt in that area. He travelled up the Saskatchewan River to Fort Edmonton and then crossed the mountains on horseback to arrive in Victoria, BC. His paintings depict scenery, Indigenous peoples, fur traders, settlers, and missionaries of the time.

• • •

Part of the historic route of the voyageurs, *Kakabeka Falls*, at forty metres high, is the second highest waterfall in Ontario after Niagara Falls. "Kakabeka" comes from the Anishinaabe word "Kah-kah-pee-kah," which means "thundering water" or "sheer cliff" or "high falls."[20]

• • •

Michael Kusugak (1948–) is an award-winning writer from Nunavut, whose children's stories mainly depict the traditional culture of the Inuit. He co-authored his first book, *A Promise is a Promise*, with bestselling author Robert Munsch.

• • •

The legend of Greenmantle

Greenmantle, the beautiful dark-eyed daughter of Chief Ogama Eagle, was beloved by the Anishinaabe people. One day, she was snatched away by Dakota warriors. Time passed. A day came when the Dakota mounted a surprise attack on the Anishinaabe. They forced Greenmantle into a canoe to guide their warriors to the Anishinaabe encampment. Pretending to be a traitor to her people, Greenmantle guided the Dakota down the Kaministiquia River to the white-water, where she suddenly swerved her canoe toward the bank, leapt out, and swam to shore. Caught in the rapids, the Dakota warriors were carried over Kakabeka Falls to perish on the rocks below. Greenmantle hurried down the portage trail to warn her people, who were then able to defeat the Dakota enemy. Some say that Greenmantle went over the falls to save her people and that her spirit lingers on as a rainbow in the mist, while the voices of the Dakota warriors crash and echo on the rocks below.[21]

L

L IS THE LOONIE,
    THE COIN WORTH ONE DOLLAR
ENGRAVED WITH A LOON
    AND ITS PARTIAL WHITE COLLAR

LACROSSE, LOONS, AND LAURIER,
    AND LAKE LOUISE,
LEDUC NO. 1
    AND LABRADOR TEAS

The one dollar coin was introduced in 1987 as a cost-saving measure to replace one dollar bills. The new coin was originally supposed to pay homage to Canada's fur trade by featuring an Indigenous person and a voyageur paddling a canoe. However, the dyes that were supposed to be used in the new coin were lost in transit between Ottawa and Winnipeg. Fearing that the lost dyes would be used to make counterfeit coins, the government settled on a new design by Robert-Ralph Carmichael. This popular coin, which features a solitary loon, was immediate dubbed "the *loonie*."

At the 2002 Olympics in Salt Lake City, Canadian icemaker Trent Evans embedded a loonie at centre ice before flooding the playing surface. It was dubbed the "lucky loonie" after both the men's and women's hockey teams won gold medals for Canada. That loonie is now in the Hockey Hall of Fame. Since that time, the Royal Canadian Mint has issued a "Lucky Loonie" coin for every Olympic and Paralympic games. Every athlete participating in the 2016 Olympics received the commemorative coin.

———————— ••• ————————

Lacrosse is one of the oldest North American sports. Originally played by First Nations people, it gained popularity with non-Indigenous people in the mid-1800s. Perhaps the most famous lacrosse game ever played was in 1763 between the Meskwaki (Fox) and the Anishinaabe at Fort Michilimackinac (originally in a section of New France that is now part of Michigan). The British troops were so enthralled with the fast action that they failed to notice Indigenous women sneaking weapons into the fort, which was then successfully overtaken by the players, who happened to be Pontiac's warriors. In 1994, lacrosse was proclaimed Canada's official summer sport.

———————— ••• ————————

Generally a solitary bird, the *common loon* is found in freshwater lakes in every province and territory of Canada. Loons are excellent swimmers, fliers, and divers, but they are clumsy on land; it is because of this clumsiness that they were given the name "loon." During the summer, the loon is a striking black and white, with a white partial necklace. Its red eyes probably help to attract a mate and to defend its territory. In the fall, loons become a plain, dull, brownish-grey colour. Their eyes also turn grey. They migrate to the Pacific and Atlantic coasts, where they easily adapt to salt water because they have special glands between their eyes that remove salt from the water and the fish they consume. Loons are flightless when they moult because they lose all of their feathers at once. Before it can return to northern lakes in the spring, the loon must grow a complete set of flight feathers to support its heavy weight. The loon has four calls—the wail, the tremolo, the yodel, and the hoot—but is usually silent in the southern wintering grounds. For many Canadians, the call of the loon is a powerful, haunting symbol of the magnificent wilderness.

> *The time will soon be here when my grandchild will long for the cry of a loon.*[22]
>
> *-Chief Dan George*

Sir Wilfrid Laurier (1841–1919) was the prime minister of Canada from 1896 to 1911. He was the first French Canadian to hold that office. A strong supporter of national unity, national autonomy, and individual rights, his portrait appears on the Canadian five-dollar bill. He claimed that "Canada is free and freedom is its nationality."[23] Laurier was known for compromise and positive thinking; the phrase "sunny ways" was first associated with his political style and, more than a century later, was adopted by Prime Minister Justin Trudeau.

Lake Louise is located in Banff National Park. A Stoney guide showed Ho-Run-Num-Nay (Lake of Little Fishes) to Tom Wilson, a CPR workman, who named it Emerald Lake. It was later renamed Lake Louise to honour the fourth daughter of Queen Victoria. The lake's turquoise colour is from the rock flour (very fine powder formed by glaciers moving over bedrock) that is suspended in the water.

Did You Know?

At 1,540 metres, Lake Louise hamlet has the highest elevation of any permanent community in Canada.

On February 13, 1947, *Leduc No. 1* struck oil in Leduc, starting the postwar oil boom in Alberta. The oilfield at Turner Valley, Alberta, was rapidly decreasing, so Imperial Oil decided to send out crews to search for other sites in Alberta and Saskatchewan. The crews had to work long shifts in bitterly cold winter conditions. One man even froze his buttocks during an eight-hour shift at the top of a rig in minus 35 degrees Celsius. The workers often slept in uninsulated sheds. When the crew was working at Leduc, distrustful townspeople refused them service in the local hotel and restaurant. Everyone was discouraged. The well on Mike Turta's farm was a last-ditch attempt to find oil, although no one expected success. After ten weeks of fruitless drilling, the crew was about to cap the well when they were ordered to drill down one more metre. And that changed everything.

— • • • —

Three species of *Labrador tea* grow in Canada. It is present in bogs, muskegs, peatlands, swamps, tundra, and coniferous woodlands as far north as the treeline, as far south as the United States, as far east as Labrador, and as far west as Alaska. It is absent from the far north and on the dry prairies. Different varieties occur in different habitats, but all three species grow in profusion in Labrador. This plant was traditionally used by Indigenous peoples to treat a variety of medical conditions, including diarrhea, migraines, arthritis, burns, and hair loss. For European settlers, it was a substitute beverage when supplies of black tea ran out. Labrador tea should be made weak, by steeping the leaves in boiling water for about five minutes. Some people consider Labrador tea to be an acquired taste.

Labrador tea dolls are steeped in Innu culture and history. Traditionally, Innu women made the dolls from caribou hides, stuffed them with a couple of pounds of loose black tea leaves, and gave them to children to carry during the biannual hunting migrations between the Labrador coast and the interior. When supply ran out, the tea was removed and the dolls re-stuffed with grasses, leaves, or moss. Labrador tea dolls are still made today (usually with a combination of caribou hide and cloth). Each designer's dolls are unique—which adds to their popularity with contemporary collectors.

M

M IS METIS,
    WHO FOUGHT SUCH FIERCE FIGHTS
BEFORE THEY SECURED
    THEIR INDIGENOUS RIGHTS

MOCCASINS, MUKLUKS,
    MEDICARE, MORRISSEAU,
MCINTOSH, MUSKEG,
    MOUNTIES, MOOSE, MOTTO

The *Metis* are people of mixed European and Indigenous ancestry who are now recognized as one of the three Indigenous groups of Canada. Metis communities with distinct cultures, customs, and languages (Michif and now-extinct Bungee) grew up along the fur-trading routes and throughout the northwest. The Metis Homeland comprises the three prairie provinces and extends into Ontario, British Columbia, the Northwest Territories, and the northern United States.

The Metis were of paramount importance in the early fur, fishing, trapping, and logging industries. They fought for Canada in the War of 1812 and all subsequent international wars. They made Western settlement possible, provided settlers and prospectors with provisions, worked farms, established ranches, and founded cities. Metis women taught newly arrived European women how to prepare and preserve local foods and also introduced them to materials and techniques for making warm winter clothes.

But when Manitoba joined Confederation, the interests of the Metis were largely ignored. The Metis had to fight hard for lands and rights in the 1860s when the Hudson's Bay Company and Britain

Metis inventions

* "arrow" sash
* beadwork to decorate clothing and leather goods
* dance steps for horses in the RCMP Musical Ride
* ice-fishing jigger
* Metis fiddle style
* Red River carts (two-wheeled carts drawn by horses or oxen)
* "Red River Jig" (Metis national anthem)
* Red River–style construction of log buildings
* York boats (inland cargo boats)

were transferring traditional Indigenous lands to Canada, and again in the 1880s when settlers were moving west onto traditional lands. Louis Riel led the Red River Resistance and, with Gabriel Dumont, the North-West Resistance. In 1885, Riel was hanged for treason, even though he was not a Canadian citizen. The Metis today are still working to secure their rights. The

Metis National Council represents the Metis both nationally and internationally.

On June 27, 2019, the Government of Canada and the Metis Nations of Alberta (MNA), Saskatchewan (MNS), and Ontario (MNO) signed the first ever Government of Canada–Metis agreements that recognize the inherent right of Metis groups to self-government, with jurisdiction and law-making power in such important areas as citizenship, governmental operations, and leadership selection. In addition, the agreements lay down processes for negotiating and recognizing other powers that relate to culture and heritage, education, environment, health care, housing, and language.

———————— ••• ————————

The *moccasins* made by Indigenous peoples of the Arctic and Plains are traditionally hard-soled, while those made in northeastern Canada have soft soles.

———————— ••• ————————

Mukluks are soft hide winter boots worn by the Inuit.

———————— ••• ————————

Tommy Douglas is considered the father of *medicare*. He was the leader of the governing Cooperative Commonwealth Federation (CCF) party, which introduced medicare to Saskatchewan on July 1, 1962. Medicare has always been unpopular with Conservative elites. When it was first introduced in Saskatchewan, the medical establishment and the insurance industry combined forces to mount an anti-medicare campaign. They railed against it on radio and in newspapers. They sent anti-medicare propaganda to every household. They made inflammatory claims: well-trained Canadian doctors would flee, leaving only inferior, untrained, foreign doctors to treat the sick; people would not be able to choose their own doctors; abortion would become compulsory; the state would commit people to mental institutions. Doctors in favour of medicare were ostracized within the medical profession; doctors opposed to medicare went on strike for nearly a month in July 1962. Nevertheless, Douglas prevailed. Despite fierce opposition from the North American medical establishment and the insurance industry, medicare spread to the rest of Canada within the next decade.

———————— ••• ————————

Norval Morrisseau (1932–2007), a legendary Anishinaabe artist, originated the pictographic or "Woodlands School" of painting. Also called "X-ray art" or "legend painting," Morrisseau's style of painting is based on traditional Anishinaabe symbols and stories, and it combines European easel painting with Anishinaabe scrolls and rock pictography. As a child, Morrisseau (whose Anishinaabe name was Miskwaabik Animiiki, "Copper Thunderbird") broke a taboo by making drawings of prehistoric pictographs and Medewiwin birch scrolls. As an adult, he continued to break taboos by painting in brilliant colours sacred stories that had

Susan A. Ross, an illustrator, painter, and printmaker from Port Arthur (now Thunder Bay), Ontario, was the niece of documentary filmmaker Robert J. Flaherty (who directed the 1922 American film *Nanook of the North*, which was filmed in Canada). She is best known for her portraits of Indigenous peoples. With Port Arthur author Sheila Burnford (who wrote the 1963 children's classic, *The Incredible Journey*), Ross spent much time in the 1960s visiting reserves to learn about the lives of Indigenous people. Ross sketched while Burnford recorded; the result was a book called *Without Reserve* (1969), written by Burnford and illustrated by Ross. *One Woman's Arctic* (1972), also written by Burnford and illustrated by Ross, was published after they travelled to Pond Inlet to study the life of the Inuit.

Ross became friends with Norval Morrisseau in the late 1950s and travelled with him to Indigenous reserves, where she painted many Indigenous peoples, providing Canada with an important historical record of Indigenous life at that time. In addition to friendship, she gave Morrisseau art supplies and a tape recorder to record Anishinaabe stories. She also helped sell his work (which he sent to her by train). Because Toronto gallery owner Jack Pollock did not drive, Susan Ross and Sheila Burnford drove him to the home of Norval Morrisseau to view Morrisseau's portfolio in 1962.

In 2002, Susan Ross was awarded the Order of Canada and Queen Elizabeth II's Golden Jubilee Medal. Ross's paintings hang in galleries across Canada. Morrisseau's pen and ink drawing of Ross (called *Susan*) is owned by the National Gallery of Canada.

previously only been passed down orally. His motivation was to keep traditional Anishinaabe culture alive and to make it relevant in the modern world.

Norval Morrisseau broke through the white-art only barrier of Canada's art scene in 1962 with his hugely successful exhibition at the Pollock Gallery in Toronto. A popular story suggests that Jack Pollock and Norval Morrisseau first met in Beardmore, a small town in northern Ontario where Pollock was teaching art classes in the summer of 1962. Pollock had heard of Morrisseau from Susan Ross (see sidebar, p. 95), but Pollock was not interested until Morrisseau showed up at the class one afternoon. Morrisseau simply walked in and plunked his paintings in front of Pollock, who was stunned by the original and passionate artwork and asked to see more. After a visit to Morrisseau's home, where Morrisseau presented more of his work and painted a picture in front of him, Pollock suggested an exhibition in Toronto. The exhibition was a smash hit and Morrisseau immediately became an important name in Canada's art world.

At various times in his frequently poverty-stricken life, Morrisseau paid with his art for meals, supplies, and liquor. Norval Morrisseau was the first Indigenous artist to gain widespread national acclaim in Canada, and he was named to the Order of Canada in 1978. To celebrate, he held a garden party for twenty-one guests, claiming, "Well, if the Queen can hold garden parties, why can't I?"[24] Each guest received an American buffalo nickel and an original Morrisseau sketch.

———————— ••• ————————

McIntosh apples are one of the most popular apple varieties grown in Canada. John McIntosh of Ontario started the brand in 1811 when he discovered, and propagated, a sapling growing on his property. The original tree bore fruit for over ninety years. Spartan apples are a hybrid of the McIntosh.

———————— ••• ————————

Muskeg is an Algonkin term for "grassy bog." Canada might have more of it than any other country. Legend has it that during construction of the CPR, rails and a railway engine were swallowed by muskeg.

———————— ••• ————————

The North-West Mounted Police (NWMP) was established in 1873. Its first accomplishment was to earn the approval of Crowfoot, Chief of the Blackfoot people, by arresting and convicting whiskey traders in present-day Alberta. The scarlet-coated *Mountie* as a symbol of Canada goes at least as far back as the 1880s. In 1920, a national police force was established, and the NWMP became the Royal Canadian Mounted Police (RCMP). The slogan "the Mountie always gets his man" has its origins in an 1877 American newspaper report. The saying was later popularized in Hollywood movies. The popular RCMP Musical Ride—an equestrian performance that is set to music and involves intricate cavalry drill manoeuvres—performs nationally and internationally, and entertains audiences in up to fifty communities across Canada each year.

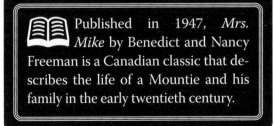

Published in 1947, *Mrs. Mike* by Benedict and Nancy Freeman is a Canadian classic that describes the life of a Mountie and his family in the early twentieth century.

Did You Know?

The RCMP Musical Ride was probably first performed in 1876 at Fort Macleod. It currently has a full troop of thirty-two cavalry, including at least two women. The Musical Ride raises money for charities and non-profit organizations, but there are free annual performances in Ottawa. These "Sunset Ceremonies" usually occur late in June. The Mounties perform the Musical Ride against the setting sun and then line up for the flag-lowering ceremony as the sun sinks below the horizon and the audience sings "O Canada."

Moose are the largest members of the deer family, and they are found everywhere in Canada except Prince Edward Island. They are excellent swimmers, and they can forage for nutrient-rich underwater plants because their nostrils act as shut-off valves to keep water out of their noses. They can also hold their breath for one minute and dive as deep as six metres. For the Anishinaabe and Cree, the moose symbolizes strength and endurance. Climate change is causing problems for moose populations because of the increased prevalence of ticks and because white-tailed deer, which carry a brain parasite that is fatal to moose, are moving north.

Moose rescues are not uncommon in Canada, but when a northern Ontario moose named Oliver was rescued, it became international news. Stephan Michel Desgroseillers and friends were out quad biking when they came across an abandoned newborn. The calf immediately bonded with them and would not go back into the woods. Fearing that it would wander onto the road, Desgroseillers took it home overnight. The next day, en route to a sanctuary, he stopped at a Tim Hortons, where the newborn was filmed making friends with customers.

———————— ••• ————————

Canada's official *motto* is *A mari usque ad mare* ("from sea to sea"). The motto comes from Psalm 72:8 in the Bible. The full phrase is "He shall have dominion also from sea to sea, and from the river unto the ends of the earth." The motto was adopted by the founding provinces of the Dominion of Canada, and the phrase did not refer to Canada's geography since the dominion did not stretch from sea to sea; British Columbia had not yet joined Confederation. Modern-day politicians appear to relate the phrase to Canada's coastlines, and they frequently use the revised "from sea to sea to sea" to refer to the entire nation.

———————— ••• ————————

N

N IS NORTHWEST PASSAGE,
 A ROUTE THAT WAS SOUGHT
SINCE IT LED TO THE EAST—
 OR SO IT WAS THOUGHT

NIAGARA, NANAIMO BARS,
 NEWFIE JOKES TOO,
NOBELS, NEWFOUNDLAND,
 AND NANABIJOU

Many early explorers searched in vain for the *Northwest Passage*, a sea corridor through Canada's Arctic waters that was believed to be a shortcut to the Orient. Roald Amundsen finally navigated it in the early 1900s. In 1940, Henry Larsen (a Canadian immigrant from Norway) sailed the *St. Roch* through the passage from Vancouver to Halifax, becoming the first to sail the Northwest Passage from west to east. Climate change is causing Arctic sea ice to melt, making the passage more navigable and thus more commercially viable. Other countries now claim that these are international waters and therefore not subject to Canada's laws.

Two famous disasters of Northwest Passage exploration are the expeditions of Henry Hudson (1610–1611) and Sir John Franklin (1845). While searching for the Northwest Passage in 1610, Hudson sailed *The Discovery* into what is now called Hudson Bay. The ship became icebound in James Bay, and, in 1611, Hudson's crew mutinied and set Hudson and eight others adrift in a small boat. Hudson was never heard from again.

The Franklin Expedition of 1845 also ended in disaster when the *Erebus* and the *Terror* and the crewmembers aboard them vanished in 1845—a disappearing act that spawned several reward offers and thirty search and rescue expeditions over the next twenty years. Lady Franklin, the wife of Sir John Franklin, outfitted five ships between 1850 and 1857 to search for her missing husband before receiving the news from the last expedition she financed that Sir John Franklin had died in 1847. The *Erebus* was finally discovered in 2014 and the *Terror* in 2016. The ships are now the joint property of Parks Canada and the Inuit (who played a large role in the discovery).

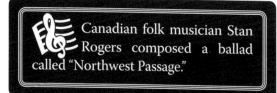

Canadian folk musician Stan Rogers composed a ballad called "Northwest Passage."

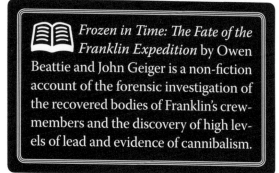

Frozen in Time: The Fate of the Franklin Expedition by Owen Beattie and John Geiger is a non-fiction account of the forensic investigation of the recovered bodies of Franklin's crewmembers and the discovery of high levels of lead and evidence of cannibalism.

By volume, *Niagara* ("Thundering Waters") is the world's greatest waterfall. The falls have moved eleven kilometres from their original location at Queenston due to the continuous erosion of the underlying limestone escarpment.

On June 30, 1859, Jean François Gravelet ("The Great Blondin") became the first tightrope walker to cross Niagara Falls. He managed to prolong the stunt for over seventeen minutes by lying down for a rest and by balancing on one leg for a time. After completing the crossing, he paused and then crossed back again more quickly. On subsequent outings, he crossed Niagara Falls blindfolded, on stilts, with manacled hands and feet, pushing a wheelbarrow, and with his manager on his back. Other stunts included somersaults and cooking an omelet on the tightrope stretched across Niagara Falls.

The first person to survive going over Niagara Falls in a barrel was American Annie Edson Taylor, who took the plunge on her sixty-third birthday on October 24, 1901.

It is now illegal to do stunts at Niagara Falls; however, in tribute to the stunting history that made Niagara Falls world famous, the Niagara Parks Commission will consider proposals by stunting professionals once in a generation (approximately once every twenty years).

Visitors have 50,000 years to visit Niagara Falls before it disappears.

The *Nanaimo bar*, a three-layer chocolat-ey dessert, originated in Nanaimo, British Columbia. Tourism Nanaimo publishes a Nanaimo Bar Trail brochure so that visitors can sample the bar's many variations.

In 1986, Joyce Hardcastle won a Nanaimo-based contest for the best Nanaimo Bar recipe with this entry.

Nanaimo Bar [25]

BOTTOM LAYER:

✱ 1/2 cup unsalted butter (European style cultured)	Melt first 3 ingredients in top of double boiler. Add egg and stir to cook and thicken. Remove from heat. Stir in crumbs, coconut, and nuts. Press firmly into an ungreased 8" x 8" pan.
✱ 1/4 cup sugar	
✱ 5 Tbsp cocoa	
✱ 1 egg, beaten	
✱ 1-1/4 cups graham wafer crumbs	
✱ 1/2 cup finely chopped almonds	
✱ 1 cup coconut	

SECOND LAYER:

✱ 1/2 cup unsalted butter	Cream butter, cream, custard powder, and icing sugar together well. Beat until light. Spread over bottom layer.
✱ 2 Tbsp and 2 tsp cream	
✱ 2 Tbsp vanilla custard powder	
✱ 2 cups icing sugar	

THIRD LAYER:

✱ 4 squares semi-sweet chocolate (1 oz. each)	Melt chocolate and butter over low heat. Cool. Once cool but still liquid, pour over second layer and chill in refrigerator.
✱ 2 Tbsp unsalted butter	

The *Newfie joke* is a distinctive form of Canadian folklore and is told by, about, and to Newfoundlanders. This is not to say that it is always *enjoyed* by Newfoundlanders. Newfie jokes are blagues (jokes that are insulting). Many people find the jokes derogatory and some Newfoundlanders find the term "Newfie" offensive as well. Here's a (relatively unobjectionable) example collected by folklorist Peter Narvaez:

A Newfoundlander living in Boston bought her old mother a telephone so that she could call her. One day the phone rang and the operator said, "Long distance from Boston." The old lady replied, "That it is," and hung up! [26]

———— ••• ————

Several Canadians have won *Nobel* prizes in chemistry, economics, literature, physics, and "physiology or medicine." In 1923, F. H. Banting and J. J. R. Macleod won the Nobel Prize in Physiology or Medicine for the discovery of insulin, one of the most important medical discoveries of all time. In 1957, Prime Minister Lester B. Pearson won the Nobel Peace Prize for his diplomatic role in resolving the Suez Crisis of 1956. Pugwash, a small town in Nova Scotia, gained instant fame when the 1995 Nobel Peace Prize was awarded to the Pugwash Conferences on Science and World Affairs in recognition of their role in nuclear disarmament. The organization first met in Pugwash because hometown tycoon Cyrus Eaton offered his spacious lodge as a venue when Albert Einstein and Bertrand Russell called for a worldwide conference on science and world peace.

———— ••• ————

In Canada, *Newfoundland and Labrador* comes first (geographically, depending on the direction of travel) and last (historically). Newfoundlanders are the first to see the sun rise on North America, because Cape Spear is the most easterly point on the continent. The province was one of the earliest European settlements in Canada (Vikings circa 1000 CE) and the last province to join Confederation (in 1949).

John Cabot landed on June 24, 1497, which was the feast of St. John the Baptist. In honour of the saint, Cabot named the "newfoundelande" St. John's Isle. Eventually, the island became known

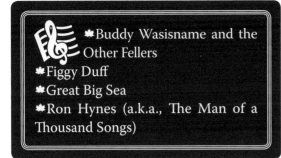

* Buddy Wasisname and the Other Fellers
* Figgy Duff
* Great Big Sea
* Ron Hynes (a.k.a., The Man of a Thousand Songs)

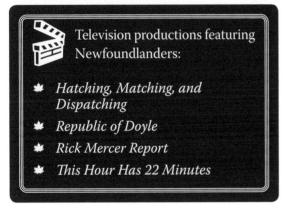

Television productions featuring Newfoundlanders:

* *Hatching, Matching, and Dispatching*
* *Republic of Doyle*
* *Rick Mercer Report*
* *This Hour Has 22 Minutes*

refined petroleum products). In addition, Newfoundlanders spend a lot of time making music, concocting clever comedies, and instructing the rest of Canada how to pronounce the province's name correctly. "Under*stand*, it's Newfound*land.*"

— ••• —

Nanabijou is the "sleeping giant" peninsula that dominates the harbour view in Thunder Bay, Ontario. According to Anishinaabe Traditional Stories, the great spirit Nanabijou was turned to stone when the location of Silver Islet was revealed to white men.

— ••• —

as Newfoundland and is often familiarly called "The Rock." The capital city became St. John's. Labrador is said to have been named "Terra del Lavrador" (land of the farmer) by Portuguese explorer Gaspar Corte-Real. The main industries of the province are fishing, mining, oil and gas, lumber, and manufacturing (boats, fish products, pulp and paper,

O IS "O CANADA,"
　　OUR NATIONAL DITTY
AND ALSO OTTAWA,
　　OUR CAPITAL CITY

OTTERS, OGOPOGO,
　　OYSTERS, AND OSPREY,
OOKPIK, OLYMPICS,
　　OPALS, OJIBWAY

"*O Canada*," the national anthem of Canada, was first performed in Quebec City in 1880. Sir Adolphe-Basile Routhier wrote the French words to the music composed by Calixa Lavallée. The French words have always remained the same, but the English words have changed many times. In 1906, Whaley and Royce Company of Toronto published Lavallée's music, Routhier's text, and an English translation by Dr. Thomas Bedford Richardson. In 1908, Mercy E. Powell McCulloch won a *Collier's Weekly* competition to rewrite the English words, but her lyrics never caught on. That same year, Ewing Buchan also had a go, as did Robert Stanley Weir. Weir's lyrics were slightly modified for the Diamond Jubilee of Confederation in 1927. Parliament proclaimed Weir's first verse as Canada's national anthem in 1980, and also, acting on the recommendations of a 1967 parliamentary committee, amended the official English words once more. "And stand on guard, O Canada" became "From far and wide, O Canada," and "O Canada, glorious and free" was changed to "God keep our land, glorious and free." In 2018, the English words were changed again to ensure gender parity. "True patriot love in all thy sons command" is now "True patriot love in all of us command."

Queen Victoria chose *Ottawa* to be the capital city of the Dominion of Canada in 1857. Parliament had previously convened in Kingston, Quebec, Montréal, and Toronto. Originally incorporated in 1850 as Bytown (after its developer, Lt. Col. John By), the site was renamed Ottawa in 1854 to mark the two hundredth anniversary of the first fur trading between the Ottawa (or Outaouais or Ondataouaouat) First Nation and the French. "Ottawa" or "Odawa" is said to be an English version of the Anishinaabe (Algonkin) word "Adàwe," which means "to trade." An Anishinaabe group called the Odawa were great intertribal traders on the Odawa River. They chiefly traded cornmeal, sunflower oil, furs, skins, rugs, mats, tobacco, and medicinal roots and herbs.

Each winter, Ottawa's Rideau Canal (a UNESCO World Heritage Site) becomes the Rideau Canal Skateway, the world's largest naturally frozen skating rink. On average, twenty thousand people visit the 7.8 kilometre skateway each winter day, many of them local commuters who skate to work or to school.

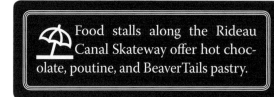

Food stalls along the Rideau Canal Skateway offer hot chocolate, poutine, and BeaverTails pastry.

—— ••• ——

Pacific Coast *sea otters* were almost completely wiped out during the fur trade. They were reintroduced to the area from 1969 to 1972 and are making a comeback there. *River otters* live throughout Canada, along rivers, lakes, and oceans. Known as playful animals, otters have excellent underwater vision, sense of smell, and sensitivity to vibrations (through their whiskers). They have no blubber; dense fur provides insulation. They can remain underwater for up to eight minutes.

Canadians have a soft spot for otters. Six otter residents (Hardy, Katmai, Kunik, Mak, Hardy, Rialto, and Tanu) at the Vancouver Aquarium showed the country how to enjoy a snow day by rolling in the white stuff and making snowballs. Otty the Otter took up the urban life in Winnipeg, where he set up housekeeping under a city dumpster. He managed to build slides to his home before being captured and relocated to the Wildlife Haven Rehabilitation Centre. An adaptable sort, he seemed to enjoy life at the centre, lazing around on soft blankets and eating frozen fish before his release into the wild, where he happily slipped into the river. An otter named Elvis earned his more notorious reputation during an infamous crime spree in Vancouver. He managed to offend several members of the local Chinese Canadian community by slipping uninvited into the walled Dr. Sun Yat-Sen Classical Chinese Garden and helping himself to several resident koi. Adding insult to injury, he also managed to steal the lures from several baited traps before escaping unscathed— almost certainly not having learned his lesson and probably with a high likelihood of reoffending elsewhere.

Otter-ly amazing, aren't they?

—————— ••• ——————

It is generally seen as green humps undulating quickly through the water. It has a long neck and either a sheep's or a horse's head. For First Nations people, N'ha-a-itk was a fierce lake monster that had to be appeased with an animal sacrifice. New Canadian settlers were very wary of it. After the 1878 sightings by Susan Allison and Thomas Smitheran, armed men patrolled the shores of Lake Okanagan to protect their families. In 1926, *The Province* newspaper announced that ferries would be fitted with protective devices to repel attacks from the sea monster. After it was given the name *Ogopogo* (from an English music-hall dance song), the monster seemed less fearsome. In 1990, Canada issued an Ogopogo stamp. (If you can neither make heads nor tails of the Okanagan monster, it might be because "Ogopogo" is a palindrome—a word that reads the same forward and backward.)

• • •

Oysters are found on both the Atlantic and Pacific coasts. Overfishing and habitat destruction greatly reduced their numbers after Europeans arrived in Canada.

Oyster facts:

❋ Oysters will change gender at least once in their lifetime.

❋ British Columbia and PEI are Canada's top producers of farmed oysters.

❋ In 1892, the maximum penalty in Canada for stealing oysters was seven years in prison.

❋ In Canada today, the maximum penalty for stealing more than $5,000 worth of oysters is ten years in prison.

• • •

The *osprey* is the official bird of Nova Scotia. Once a threatened species due to heavy human use of pesticides, since the banning of DDT ospreys have made a comeback, and they inhabit water landscapes across Canada. Ospreys play an important role as an umbrella species because they reflect the overall health of an aquatic environment. These carnivorous birds have a white head with a black eye stripe. Ninety-nine percent of their diet is wild fish. Adept at soaring and diving, they are extremely successful hunters,

Well, shucks, Canadians really are good at opening oysters.

❋**Guinness World Record:**
Patrick McMurray; 39 oysters in 1 minute; June 5, 2017

❋**Guinness World Record:**
Canadian Team (Josh Bishop, Janet Hardy Callaghan, Eamon Clark, Philip Ho, Mike Langley, Patrick McMurray, Daniel Notkin, Simeron Novak, Jeff Noye, and Jesse Papastavros); 8,840 oysters in one hour; July 31, 2014

averaging twelve minutes to make a catch. The barbed pads on the soles of their feet help them grip slippery fish. While in flight, ospreys orient fish headfirst to lessen wind resistance. Ospreys usually lay three eggs, which both the male and the female incubate. Ospreys stagger the eggs, laying them one to three days apart. Because incubation begins immediately with the first egg, the eggs all hatch at different times. With ospreys, the early bird does catch the worm. Older siblings are stronger and more dominant than younger siblings. In times of food scarcity, the older siblings take all of the food, leaving the younger siblings to starve.

One-third of the world's ospreys live in Canada—often at the tops of dead trees or electrical transmission poles (which pose an electrocution, fire, and entanglement hazard). Hydro crews across the country frequently relocate ospreys that have chosen hydro poles as their homes.

••••

The *Ookpik* (from the Inuktitut word "ukpik," which means "snowy owl" or "Arctic owl") was a popular Canadian souvenir in the 1960s. Made of sealskin, it is a small stuffed toy with a large head and big eyes. It was first created by Jeannie Snowball in 1963 at the Fort Chimo Eskimo Cooperative (now Kuujjuaq Co-op) in Quebec and was Canada's mascot at a 1964 Philadelphia trade fair. Its arrival at the fair was preceded by mysterious posters announcing "Ookpik is coming." Even though the Ookpik was a mascot—and not a product—the Canadian government received twelve thousand cash orders for it. Its popularity soared and it had a strong presence at the Centennial celebrations. At the height of its popularity, the Ookpik was receiving one hundred fan letters each week. Al Beaton wrote an Ookpik comic that for two years was syndicated in fifty newspapers. Some newspaper editorials suggested that the Ookpik should be featured on Canada's new flag. By the late 1960s, the fad was over. The Ookpik disappeared, a victim of overpricing at Expo 67 and of the growing worldwide anti-sealing movement.

••••

Three Canadian cities have hosted the *Olympic Games*: Montréal (1976), Calgary (1988), and Vancouver (2010).

In Montréal, Queen Elizabeth II watched her daughter, Princess Anne, compete in individual show jumping; American Bruce (now Caitlyn) Jenner became a North American household name by winning gold in decathlon; and fourteen-year-old Nadia Comaneci of Romania became the first gymnast ever to score a perfect ten.

In Calgary, Canadians mourned Brian Orser's silver medal in men's figure skating at the same time they exulted in Elizabeth Manley's silver in women's figure skating; and "Eddie the Eagle" of England stole the Olympic show by finishing last in ski jumping and cheerfully asserting that the Olympics are not just for winners.

In Vancouver, the games got off to a tragic start when Georgian luge athlete Nodar Kumaritashvili died in a training run at Whistler Sliding Centre. Alexandre Bilodeau became the first Canadian ever to win Olympic gold in Canada when, in honour of his brother who has cerebral palsy, he won the gold medal in men's freestyle skiing–moguls. Showing strength in the face of adversity, Joannie Rochette of Canada won bronze in women's figure skating two days after the sudden death of her mother.

The gemstone *opal* is mined in the Okanagan area of British Columbia. The "queen of gemstones" is October's official birthstone. It is formed by rain, which seeps into rock crevasses and then evaporates, leaving silica deposits that harden into opal. Opal is the only gemstone that can contain every colour in the rainbow. The word "opal" has Greek and Latin origins. "Opallios" (Greek) means "to see a change of colour" and "opalus" (Latin) means "precious stone."

Visitors can dig for opals at the Klinker Opal Mine in British Columbia. On one dig, tourist Donna Nelson discovered a rock bearing multiple opals—a find worth close to $3,000.

———————— ••• ————————

The *Ojibway* are one of the largest First Nations groups in Canada. They are also called Saulteaux, Mississauga, or Chippewa, but they identify themselves as Anishinaabe ("one of the people" or "original people"). Traditionally, they lived in the Eastern Woodlands and were important participants in the fur trade. The Anishinaabe people believe that their ancestors were originally placed on the continent by the Creator. Other fundamental beliefs are unity and the oneness of all things.

———————— ••• ————————

Traditional Anishinaabe culture includes

* **beadwork**: traditional, colourful, ornate decorative art on garments, jewelry, moccasins, teepees.

* **birchbark**: the bark of birch trees used for canoes, dwellings (wigwams), mats, objects (baskets, bowls, cookware, food storage containers), religious scrolls, toys.

* **canoes**: primary means of transportation in seasons other than winter.

* **copper**: used for tools (awls, chisels, fishhooks, knives, wedges), weapons (spear points) and jewelry (beads, bracelets, rings).

* **cowrie shells**: smooth, shiny seashells (acquired from the ground or on the shores of lakes and rivers or through a vast and ancient trading network) used in ceremonies and for trade.

* **maple syrup**: traditional food, beverage, and seasoning used in liquid form or made into maple sugar.

* **moccasins**: soft leather shoes (usually deerskin) that vary in design and decoration between bands.

* **Powwows**: communal celebrations of Indigenous culture (art, dance, drums, history, music, song).

* **snowshoes**: primary means of travel across snow during the winter.

* **Sweat Lodges**: simple round structures constructed for spiritual cleansing or purification ceremonies.

* **teepees**: A-shaped dwellings of plains people made from the hides of bison.

* **wigwams**: domed birchbark dwellings of woodlands peoples.

* **wild rice**: food staple growing in the waters in the Great Lakes region which was often harvested by canoe and made into bread flour or cooked and added to soups.

P

P IS POUTINE,
    A SNACK SURE TO PLEASE,
IT'S FRENCH FRIES AND GRAVY
    ALL COVERED WITH CHEESE

PARLIAMENT, PETERSON,
    PARKA, AND PORCUPINE,
POLAR BEARS, PROVINCES,
    PABLUM, AND PINE

Poutine (slang for "mess") is a French Canadian snack consisting of french fries topped with cheese curds and gravy. It was first served in Quebec snack bars in the 1950s and became popular throughout Canada in the 1990s.

———— ••• ————

According to Canada's constitution, *Parliament* refers to three institutions: the Crown, the House of Commons, and the Senate. All three bodies must approve a bill before it can become law. Section 91 of the 1867 Constitution Act gives Parliament the general power to legislate matters for the "peace, order, and good government" of Canada. This power means that the federal government can pass laws on matters that would normally be provincial concerns. There are four aspects: residuary power, national dimension, emergency power, and federal paramountcy. In theory, the power is used only in emergency situations. It was used to justify the War Measures Act in the First World War (by Robert Borden), in the Second World War (by William Lyon Mackenzie King), and during the October Crisis in 1970 (by Pierre Trudeau). In reality, federal governments sometimes try to use it in non-emergency situations. An example is the 1975 Anti-Inflation Act (by Pierre Trudeau).

———— ••• ————

Montréal's *Oscar Peterson* (1925–2007) overcame arthritis and tuberculosis to become Canada's first jazz star and one of the world's all-time great jazz pianists. In his six-decade career he released more than two hundred recordings, performed as a virtuoso soloist, and collaborated with the world's premier jazz musicians, including Louis Armstrong, Count Basie, Ray Charles, Duke Ellington, Ella Fitzgerald, Stan Getz, Dizzy Gillespie, and Stéphane Grappelli.

In addition to composing and performing, Oscar Peterson taught and inspired countless music students (including Diana Krall), and he became an adjunct professor of music at York University. He was a Companion of the Order of Canada and the first recipient of the Governor General's Performing Arts Award. Other awards included thirteen consecutive *Downbeat* awards, the Glenn Gould Prize (1993), the Praemium Imperiale from the Japan Arts Association (1999), and the UNESCO International Music Prize

(2000). Throughout his illustrious career, Peterson also received worldwide acclaim for his extensive body of compositions. He composed "Hymn to Freedom" (which became the anthem of the American civil rights movement of the 1960s) and the famous *Canadiana Suite* (which he described as a musical portrait of Canada), as well as music for numerous films and documentaries, including the musical score for the film *The Silent Partner* (for which he won the Canadian Film Award for Best Original Score in 1978).

Did You Know?

❋ Peterson's extraordinary piano technique earned him the nickname "the brown bomber of boogie-woogie," and Duke Ellington called him the "Maharaja of the keyboard."

❋ In 2005, Oscar Peterson became the first living person (apart from a reigning monarch) to be featured on a Canadian stamp when Canada Post issued a 50 cent stamp in his honour.

Oscar's achievements

❋ **1997:** Grammy, Lifetime Achievement Award

❋ **1990:** Grammy, Best Jazz Instrumental Performance, Group: *Live At The Blue Note*

❋ **1987:** Juno, Best Jazz Album: *If You Could See Me Now.*

❋ **1990; 1979; 1978:** Grammy, Best Jazz Instrumental Performance, Soloist: *Montreaux '77—Oscar Peterson Jam; The Legendary Oscar Peterson Trio Live At The Blue Note; Jousts*

❋ **1978:** Canadian Music Hall of Fame induction.

❋ **1977:** Grammy, Best Jazz Performance by a Soloist: *The Giants.*

❋ **1974:** Grammy, Best Jazz Performance by a Group: *The Trio.*

A *parka* is an Inuit winter coat with a fur-lined hood and drawstrings that trap body heat inside. It is traditionally constructed of caribou skins. Historically, styles varied between different Inuit communities. Mothers carried small children inside the parka, either on their backs or inside the hoods.

———————— ••• ————————

After the beaver, the *porcupine* is Canada's next largest rodent. When frightened or cornered, it lashes out with its tail to release barbed quills or spines, which then regrow. A single porcupine can have more than thirty thousand quills, which have antibiotic properties, and a rosette on their backs that produces a strong scent that humans and predators do not like. Porcupines have big appetites and they often crave salt. They eat fruit, leaves, blossoms, water lilies, corn, berries, bark, stems, and, sometimes, canoe paddles and axe handles. The male has an unusual mating ritual that requires screaming, grunting, purring, and soaking the female in urine.

———————— ••• ————————

Based on a variety of criteria, *polar bears* are generally considered the largest bears on earth, and they live on sea ice in Canada's North. Their black skin covers a layer of fat that can be 11.5 centimetres thick. The fat keeps the polar bear warm in Arctic sea waters; on land, their thick fur conserves heat. Although their fur looks white, it actually has no pigment. Polar bears are very vulnerable to changes in their habitat, and people fear for their future as sea ice melts. The polar bear appears on the two-dollar coin in Canada.

———————— ••• ————————

Pablum was developed in 1930 by pediatricians Theodore Drake (1891–1959), Frederick Tisdall (1893–1949), and Alan Brown (1887–1960) at Toronto's Hospital for Sick Children to improve the nutrition of young children. Because Pablum contained calcium and vitamin D, it helped prevent rickets. It is called "Pablum" because the Latin word for food is "pabulum."

———————— ••• ————————

Pine is the most common conifer in Canada and was the most sought-after tree for logging. After Napoleon blockaded the Baltic in the early 1800s, the British imported Canadian pine to make masts for navy ships. During the next centuries, pine lumber was also used to build, furnish, and paper North American cities.

Some pines are fire-resistant or fire-dependent. The pitch pine can re-sprout even if its main trunk has been burnt. The Jack pine needs fire to propagate. When fire melts the resin covering the cones, the seeds are released.

The Haudenosaunee (Iroquois) call the Great White Pine the Tree of Peace.

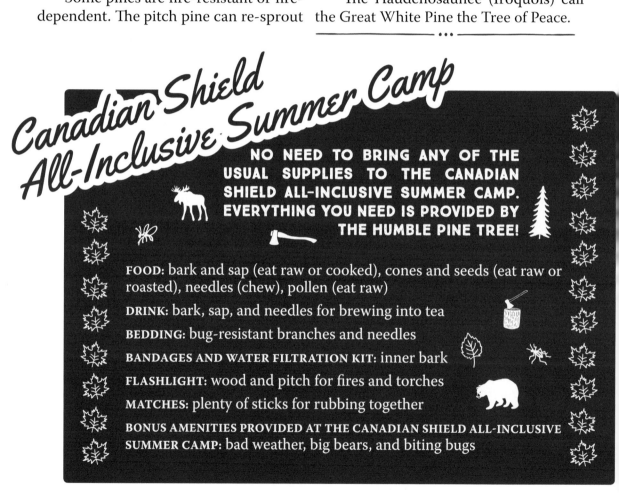

Canadian Shield All-Inclusive Summer Camp

NO NEED TO BRING ANY OF THE USUAL SUPPLIES TO THE CANADIAN SHIELD ALL-INCLUSIVE SUMMER CAMP. EVERYTHING YOU NEED IS PROVIDED BY THE HUMBLE PINE TREE!

FOOD: bark and sap (eat raw or cooked), cones and seeds (eat raw or roasted), needles (chew), pollen (eat raw)

DRINK: bark, sap, and needles for brewing into tea

BEDDING: bug-resistant branches and needles

BANDAGES AND WATER FILTRATION KIT: inner bark

FLASHLIGHT: wood and pitch for fires and torches

MATCHES: plenty of sticks for rubbing together

BONUS AMENITIES PROVIDED AT THE CANADIAN SHIELD ALL-INCLUSIVE SUMMER CAMP: bad weather, big bears, and biting bugs

Canada has ten *provinces* and three territories

PROVINCE OR TERRITORY	ENTRY INTO CONFEDERATION	CAPITAL CITY	LICENSE PLATE TAGLINE
Alberta	1905	Edmonton	Wild Rose Country
British Columbia	1871	Victoria	Beautiful British Columbia
Manitoba	1870	Winnipeg	Friendly Manitoba
New Brunswick	1867	Fredericton	New Nouveau Brunswick
Newfoundland and Labrador	1949	St. John's	Newfoundland Labrador
Northwest Territories	1870	Yellowknife	Spectacular Northwest Territories
Nova Scotia	1867	Halifax	Canada's Ocean Playground
Nunavut	1999	Iqaluit	ᓄᓇᕗᑦ Nunavut
Ontario	1867	Toronto	A Place to Grow (personal) Open for Business (commercial)
Prince Edward Island	1873	Charlottetown	Birthplace of Confederation
Quebec	1867	Quebec	Je me souviens
Saskatchewan	1905	Regina	Land of Living Skies
Yukon	1898	Whitehorse	The Klondike

Q

Q IS QUEBEC
    AND ALSO THE QUEEN,
TWO FOUNDING NATIONS
    CAN CLEARLY BE SEEN

QUEUES DE CASTOR,
    QUEEN'S PLATE, AND QUETICO,
QUARRIES, QUARTZ, QUILLWORK,
    QUINZHEE, QUATSINO

In 1969, the Official Languages Act made Canada officially a bilingual country. Equality of French and English rights in Canada stems from the notion that in Canada there are two founding nations—the French and the English. Most French-speaking Canadians live in the province of *Quebec* (an Algonkin word meaning "where the river narrows"). In 1985 Quebec City (originally called Stadacona by the Iroquoian-speaking locals) was named a UNESCO World Heritage Site.

•••

Her Majesty Queen Elizabeth II (1926–) formally became *Queen of Canada* in 1953. She is fluently bilingual in French and English.

•••

Queues de Castor or BeaverTails is an international chain of pastry stands. From its beginnings in 1978 when Pam and Grant Hooker introduced Canadians to the pastries at the Killaloe Fair, the chain quickly spread across Ontario into Quebec and then, in the 1990s, appeared in locations across Canada, the United States, and abroad. Queues de Castor specialize in deep-fried pastry dough, which is hand-stretched to resemble a beaver's tail and covered with sweet toppings. The company boasts of friends in high places: both President Barack Obama (on his first official visit to Canada) and Canadian astronaut Chris Hadfield (on the ground) have enjoyed the pastry.

•••

Canada's Triple Crown in horse racing consists of a series of three races: the *Queen's Plate*, the Prince of Wales Stakes, and the Breeders' Stakes. Dating from 1860, the Queen's Plate (or the King's Plate, depending on the sex of the English

- ❦ **Winner of the first purse:** Charles Littlefield Jr. riding Don Juan, 1860
- ❦ **First filly to win:** Brunette, 1864
- ❦ **First winning female jockey:** Emma-Jayne Wilson riding Mike Fox, 2007
- ❦ **Most famous champion:** Northern Dancer, who in 1964 also came first in the Kentucky Derby and the Preakness Stakes and third in the Belmont Stakes. Northern Dancer was also the most successful studhorse in the history of horse racing.

monarch) is Canada's oldest thoroughbred horse race and North America's longest continuously run thoroughbred stakes race. The trophy for the "Gallop for the Guineas" is a gold cup, and the winning jockey's gift from the Queen of England is a royal purple bag containing fifty gold sovereigns.

• • •

Quetico Provincial Park is a wilderness park in Ontario that contains more than two thousand lakes and 460,000 hectares of remote wilderness. Together with Minnesota's Boundary Waters Canoe Area Wilderness, Quetico Provincial Park makes up the largest international area in the world set aside for wilderness recreation. It is famous for backcountry canoeing and fishing.

There is some confusion over the meaning of the word "quetico." Some say it comes from the French "quête de la côte" (quest for the coast); some say it is an abbreviation of QUebec TImber COmpany, although there is no official record of such a company; some First Nations say that it comes from the Anishinaabe name given to a benevolent spirit who lives in and protects the forest.

Quetico wildlife includes: bats, beavers, birds (150 species, including bald eagles, blue jays, chickadees, ducks, grouse, loons, osprey, peregrine falcons, ravens, shorebirds, songbirds, and whisky jacks), black bears, bobcats, chipmunks, coyotes, deer, fishers, flying squirrels, foxes, hares, lynx, mink, moles, moose, muskrats, otters, pine martens, rabbits, raccoons, shrews, squirrels, and wolves.

In Quetico Provincial Park, there is no cellphone coverage, motorized boats are not permitted and there are no restaurants or lodges. Whatever is packed in must be packed out again. Quetico's pictographs (paintings on rocks) of canoes, moose, turtles, and hunters are sacred.

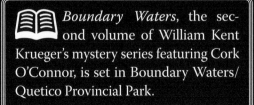

Boundary Waters, the second volume of William Kent Krueger's mystery series featuring Cork O'Connor, is set in Boundary Waters/ Quetico Provincial Park.

Canada's *quarries* are primarily limestone, followed by granite, and then marble and sandstone. Quarries in Canada are often owned and operated by construction companies who extract rock by blasting, cutting, and digging it out of large open pits. Approximately two-thirds of quarried stone is crushed for use in construction. Almost all of Canada's quarried material comes from Ontario and Quebec, and the rest mainly from British Columbia and Manitoba, which is the world's only source of Tyndall stone (dolomitic limestone). This dimensional stone is often used for walls, fireplaces, steps, and trim.

Did You Know?

* Canada's parliament buildings are constructed of Nepean sandstone from a quarry in Nepean Township in Ottawa.
* Canada has some ancient quarries:
  * Fleur de Lys Soapstone Quarries in Newfoundland and Labrador is a National Historic Site of Canada that contains evidence of quarrying techniques used by the Dorset people, who occupied the area from approximately 500 BCE to 500 CE. The Dorset people used soapstone for carving and for making various containers, including bowls and oil lamps.
  * The Quarry of the Ancestors, located near Fort McMurray, Alberta, was a source of Beaver River Silicified Sandstone (BRSS). Indigenous peoples probably discovered the sandstone deposits soon after the draining of Lake Agassiz around ten thousand years ago. They used BRSS for tools and projectile points.
* Canada's quarries are proof of reincarnation:
  * The Butchart Gardens, a National Historic Site of Canada located near Victoria, BC, is a former limestone quarry.
  * The Don Valley Brickworks (Evergreen Brick Works), a former clay and slate quarry and brickworks factory, is now a Toronto city park.
  * A former limestone quarry, St. Mary's Swimming Quarry in Ontario, is Canada's largest freshwater swimming hole. Surrounded by limestone outcrops, its waters range in depth from ten to thirty feet.

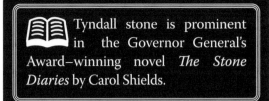

Tyndall stone is prominent in the Governor General's Award–winning novel *The Stone Diaries* by Carol Shields.

Buildings featuring Tyndall stone:

* Canadian Embassy (Berlin)
* Canadian Museum for Human Rights (Winnipeg)
* Canadian Museum of History (Gatineau)
* Fairmont Empress Hotel (Victoria)
* Manitoba Legislature (Winnipeg)
* Parliament Buildings (Ottawa)

•••

British Columbia, Manitoba, Northwest Territories, Nova Scotia, Nunavut, Ontario, Quebec, and Yukon. Amethyst, a variety of quartz, is the official gemstone of Ontario. It was discovered by accident in the Thunder Bay area during construction of a road to a fire tower.

Did You Know?

Quartz is used in clocks and watches because it is piezoelectric (which means that when pressure is applied to quartz, it produces a tiny volt of electricity; if a voltage is applied to quartz, it will vibrate). Inside a quartz clock or watch, a battery sends electricity along an electronic circuit to a piece of quartz; the quartz vibrates; the circuit then measures the vibrations and uses them to produce regular electric pulses that can turn the gears that spin the hands on the clock.

•••

Quartz is made up of silica and oxygen and is one of the most common minerals on the planet. It is present in gneiss, granite, and sandstone. It has a hardness of seven on the Mohs scale and can scratch glass and steel. It does not easily dissolve. In Canada, quartz is mined in Porcupine quill embroidery, or *quillwork*, has traditionally been done by First Nations women, who use it to decorate birchbark boxes, calumets (long-stemmed ceremonial pipes), clothing, moccasins, and teepees.

•••

A *quinzhee* is a traditional northern Indigenous snow shelter made with light, fluffy snow. Intended for temporary use, the quinzhee is built by making a mound of snow, packing it, and then hollowing it out to make a domed chamber inside. The insulating property of snow keeps inside temperatures above freezing. Important structures for winter survival, quinzhees are popular with winter campers and can save lives in emergency situations. Most Canadian children have made quinzhees. They call them snow forts.

———————— ••• ————————

Quatsino ("the downstream people" or "close to the ocean") is a First Nation, a hamlet, a sound, and a wilderness provincial park on north Vancouver Island. With the arrival of Europeans in the 1890s, many Quatsino people died from European diseases. European arrival also caused the destruction of old-growth forests, the loss of wildlife, and the pollution of lands and rivers. In 1972, the surviving members of the Quatsino First Nation were relocated to a reserve near Coal Harbour.

———————— ••• ————————

R

R IS THE RAILROAD
    THAT RUNS THROUGH THE LAND
O'ER ROCKIES AND RIVERS
    AND VAST RUPERT'S LAND

ROTARY SNOWPLOWS,
    THE ROBERTSON SCREW,
RADIO, ROLLERS,
    RICHARD, RICHELIEU

Canadian *Railroad* Questionnaire:

1. *The Canadian Pacific Railway (CPR) was Canada's first public railway.*

   FALSE. The 1836 Champlain and St. Lawrence Railroad was Canada's first public railroad.

2. *The public viewed the railroad with distrust.*

   FALSE. The public loved the new railroad, held picnics along the tracks, and walked on top of moving carriages. The picnickers often caused delays in the train schedules. The railroad company also had to introduce penalties for those who walked on top of the cars or who smuggled dogs into first-class compartments.

3. *The Canadian government issued railway charters to two companies only: the Canadian Pacific Company and the Canadian National Company.*

   FALSE. More than 2,500 railway company charters were issued in Canada after the middle of the nineteenth century. Development was haphazard, with too many companies receiving charters for the same regions, many going bankrupt, and most plundering the public purse. Eventually, many of the smaller lines amalgamated to form Canadian National Railways.

4. *Special trains brought services and entertainment to remote areas of Canada.*

   TRUE. From the 1920s to the 1960s, monthly school trains brought a teacher and a boxcar school to the children of miners, railway workers, and trappers in remote northern areas of Ontario. School trains would usually stop in a location for one week at a time. Circus, dental, and ski trains also brought entertainment and services to people.

5. *Railways played a small role in the industrialization and development of Canada.*

   FALSE. Early railways were crucial to nation building. The railroads extended into new territories and pushed the agricultural, mining, and forestry frontiers northward and westward. The CPR opened the Canadian west, bringing goods, communication, military troops, and new immigrants. Railways provided employment, galvanized heavy and service industries, stimulated engineering feats, and inspired new inventions. The railways created new demands for natural resources (wood, iron, steel), locomotives, and real estate.

6. *Railroads stimulated the development of international standard time.*

TRUE. When railways were first introduced, each community along the rail lines kept its own time according to the position of the sun. This caused confusion in train schedules and was also a safety concern since it could result in two trains being on the same track at the same time. After Sandford Fleming spent an uncomfortable night in a train station due to scheduling problems, he apparently came up with the idea of international standard time.

7. *Railways influenced the development and shape of cities.*

TRUE. New cities sprang up as service and maintenance centres for the railroads. Some cities—like Toronto—became prominent because they were hubs for several railway lines. The railroads determined the shape of cities. Railway stations were the core of urban centres, surrounded by hotels, industries, and shops.

8. *The Underground Railroad was a north-south branch of the CPR.*

FALSE. The Underground Railroad tended to run south to north, and it was not a physical train running on real rails. The Underground Railroad was a secret network of people who opposed slavery and who, at great risk, helped thirty to forty thousand Black people escape slavery in the United States and "follow the drinking gourd" to Canada. The decade from 1850 to 1860 was particularly busy for the Railroad, with fifteen to twenty thousand Black people arriving in Canada during those years. The Underground Railroad was North America's largest anti-slavery movement, and it was active until 1865, when slavery was banned in the United States.

9. *Canadian railways played a role in the anti-slavery movement in North America.*

TRUE. The anti-slavery movement happened around the time the railroad arrived in North America. Escaped slaves did sometimes travel by train, and the railroad became the main metaphor for the anti-slavery movement. The abolitionists used railway terms as a secret code to pass information without arousing suspicion from authorities.

10. *Canadian railway companies refused to hire Black workers.*

FALSE. In the late 1800s, African Canadians were employed as track layers for the CPR and as cooks and dining car attendants for the Grand Trunk Railway. The CPR actively recruited Black people to work in the rail industry (particularly as porters after the arrival of Pullman sleeping cars) and hired people from Black settlement areas in Canada (Africville in Halifax, Little Burgundy in Montréal, and the Bloor and Bathurst areas of Toronto), the United States, and the Caribbean. More than five hundred Black porters arrived to work for the CPR in Canada between 1916 and 1919. The CPR provided recruits with CPR business cards, which were then presented to Canadian border guards who were otherwise reluctant to admit Blacks into Canada.

One of the few Canadian jobs available to Black men, the position of porter

Underground Railroad terminology

* **Cargo/Freight/Package/Passengers** = escaped slaves

* **Conductors** = guides assisting fugitives

* **Depots/Stations** = safe houses providing food, lodging, clothing, money for escaped slaves

* **The Drinking Gourd** = the Big Dipper (the constellation with pointer stars leading to Polaris, the North Star)

* **Follow the Drinking Gourd** = travel north to free American states or Canada

* **Heaven/Promised Land** = free American states or Canada

* **Lines** = the routes used

* **Station Masters** = people running safe houses

* **Terminals** = towns or cities where safe houses were located

* **Ticket Agents** = the people who planned safe trips, made travel arrangements, and contacted station masters .

carried prestige in Black communities. The Canadian railway companies preferred Black men for positions as sleeping car porters because many Black people were former American slaves with extensive domestic service experience and many were well-educated. Unfortunately, the meritocratic ideals of the rail companies went no further than the observation of work of high quality. Unwanted aspects of the job for workers included: abuse from passengers; lower pay than white counterparts; on call twenty-four hours per day; unassigned sleeping quarters; no hope for promotion; no chance to apply for the positions of engineer or conductor; and no right to join unions.

In 1917, four Black porters (John A. Robinson, J. W. Barber, B. F. Jones, and P. White) formed North America's first Black railway union—the Order of Sleeping Car Porters—which later joined the Canadian Brotherhood of Railway Employees. Some negotiated benefits included: better pay; better working and sleeping conditions; fairer disciplinary practices; monthly salary increases; overtime pay; vacation time; and the right to post their names on the

Well-known African Canadians who worked for the railroad

* **Stanley G. Grizzle** (porter; first Black citizenship judge)
* **Elijah McCoy** (fireman; inventor and engineer of dual American/Canadian citizenship who invented the McCoy lubricator, which oils running machinery and was called "the real McCoy" to distinguish it from inferior imitations)
* **Rufus Rockhead** (porter; owner of Montréal jazz club Rockhead's Paradise)

sleeping cars they attended. (Many passengers disrespectfully referred to porters as "boy" or "George," after George Pullman who invented the sleeping car.)

In 1954, George V. Garraway became the first Black Canadian train conductor.

11. *The CPR had a temporary foreign worker program.*

TRUE. Between 1881 and 1884, close to seventeen thousand Chinese men were hired as temporary labourers to help build Canada's national railway. They were paid $1.00 a day, and out of those wages they had to purchase their own equipment, food, and camping and cooking supplies. (White workers were paid $1.50 to $2.50 per day and were given free tools and supplies for survival.) The temporary Chinese labour force supplied around six thousand of the seven thousand men needed to construct the fifteen tunnels through the Fraser Canyon. Chinese workers were given the most difficult and dangerous jobs of clearing and grading the railway's roadbed and blasting the rock to create the tunnels. Many perished on the job. They died in accidents, fires, dynamite blasts, and landslides. They died from malnutrition, illness, and hypothermia. They died from lack of proper medical care. They died from poor living and working conditions. For each mile through the Fraser Canyon, four Chinese men were felled.

12. *The CPR played a pivotal role in establishing the Canadian Prairies as the world's breadbasket and in settling the West.*

TRUE. The CPR ensured that Canadian grain reached the national and international markets. The CPR also made possible the timely harvest of wheat. From 1890 to 1929, when farms required large numbers of workers and wheat fields were expanding faster than the prairie population, the CPR recruited harvesters from eastern Canada, the United States, and Britain and provided special harvest excursion trains to transport them to farms in western Canada. Adventurers, clerks, drifters, factory workers, miners, professors, students, and even some experienced farmhands paid fifteen dollars for a ticket from any station in eastern Canada to Winnipeg. The CPR had no trouble attracting farm workers because farmers provided free room and board and they paid good wages: in the 1920s, harvesters could make $1.75 to $2.25 for a ten- to twelve-hour day, and threshers could make $2.00 to $3.25 each day.

In the 1920s, an estimated thirty-nine thousand people per year travelled west on the harvest excursions, with some years seeing over fifty thousand. The harvest trains set off from Toronto and Montréal and had at least twenty cars and more than twelve hundred passengers. Each car had a small stove and one toilet for approximately sixty people, who were crowded onto wooden benches for the four- to five-day journey. There were separate cars for males, females (harvesters and teachers), and Cape Bretoners, who were known for playing violins and accordions, step-dancing, drinking, and smashing windows. In 1921, at the request of the CPR, the RCMP accompanied the harvest excursions because of widespread incidents of drunkenness, theft, vandalism, riots, and harassment of female passengers on the trains.

In 1929, the stock market crashed. By 1930, the wheat economy collapsed, and the Depression and dust bowls of the 1930s meant that there was little to harvest. When conditions improved, farms became mechanized and harvest trains were no longer needed.

13. *Railways had no role to play in wartime.*

FALSE. In peace or in war, railways were at the centre of the nation's activities. In 1885, the CPR moved troops west to deal with the Northwest Resistance. During the First and Second World Wars, trains transported troops and military supplies across the country to Halifax, where they were then shipped overseas.

14. *Railways were unimportant during the Great Depression of the 1930s.*

FALSE. During the Great Depression of the 1930s, hobos "rode the rails" illegally, hopping on and off freight trains in their search for work. In 1935, during the ill-fated "On to Ottawa Trek," strikers at unemployment relief camps in British Columbia headed to Ottawa by train to protest poor working and living conditions.

15. *The last spike of the CPR is in Craigellachie, British Columbia, and the first spike is in Thunder Bay, Ontario.*

TRUE. Both spikes were made of iron. The plan was for the Governor General to bring a silver spike to the last spike ceremony, but bad weather (imagine that!) prevented him from attending. It is unknown whether Lord Lansdowne would have hammered the spike correctly in one try. CPR company director Donald A. Smith needed two tries because the first spike bent. (Pieces of the bent spike were later reproduced as decorative pins.) In the end, four last spikes were needed: the first, made of silver, did not arrive; the second was bent and replaced with the third, which became the actual ceremonial spike; the fourth was a replacement of the ceremonial spike to spoil any plans souvenir hunters might have been hatching to steal the actual ceremonial spike.

16. *The world's fastest silk routes were Canada's railways.*

TRUE. Beginning in the 1890s, for approximately fifty years, high-speed trains with armed guards carried silkworm cocoons from the harbour in Vancouver to silk mills in New York and New Jersey. Silk trains had the right of way over all other trains.

17. *Canada's railways started a boom in the tourist and travel industries.*

TRUE. Because the railroad created employment opportunities, people could afford vacations. Travel was easier and previously remote locations became accessible. From the late 1880s onwards, the railways opened commercial art departments that produced spectacular images of Canada as a desirable place to take a holiday. The CPR was particularly successful in exploiting these images at home and abroad. It expanded its operations to include hotels, steamships, telegraph services, and, eventually, an airline. The CPR became not only a means of transportation, but also a destination. Tourists travelled from afar to stay at CPR-owned Chateau Lake Louise and the Banff Springs Hotel.

18. *VIA Rail was formed when the CPR and the CNR amalgamated their passenger services.*

TRUE. By the 1950s and 1960s, more people were using automobiles and airplanes, and passenger train traffic was decreasing. In 1978, the CPR and the CNR combined their passenger services to form VIA Rail.

19. *Canada has a long tradition of funeral trains.*

TRUE. The tradition of funeral trains for political figures that began with John A. Macdonald in 1891 was very much alive in 2000, when the remains of former Prime Minister Pierre Elliott Trudeau were transported by train from Ottawa to Montréal, so people could pay their last respects along the railway line.

20. *The railways are responsible for many stereotypical images of Canada.*

TRUE. Even though rail travel was often crowded, uncomfortable, tiring, and dirty, the railroads managed to portray an image of exotic, luxurious travel. The 1939 Royal Tour, which incorporated a lot of rail travel, contributed to this image, but it was railway advertisements that created the stereotypes and mythologies about travel in Canada that still persist today in the popular imagination. The brochures and pamphlets featured mountains, Mounties, prairies, and seashores as exotic locales full of romance and wonder. Present-day railway advertisements are still filled with alluring photographs of pristine prairies, rushing rivers, and majestic mountains.

———— ••• ————

Canadian train songs

* "49 Tons" (Fred Eaglesmith)
* "Canadian Railroad Trilogy" (Gordon Lightfoot)
* "Didn't Hear the Train" (Barra MacNeils)
* "The Flyin' CPR" (Stompin' Tom Connors)
* "The Guysborough Train" (Stan Rogers)
* "Never Did Like That Train" (Murray McLauchlan)
* "Orangedale Whistle" (Jimmy Rankin)
* "Railway Tune" (James Keelaghan)

The Canadian portion of the Rocky Mountains (North America's largest mountain system) stretches 1,200 kilometres across Alberta and British Columbia from the forty-ninth parallel to the Liard River Basin. There are three passes through the *Rockies*: the Crowsnest Pass, the Yellowhead Pass, and the Kicking Horse Pass. The highest mountain in the Canadian Rockies is Mount Robson at 3,954 metres.

———— ••• ————

Canada has more than 8,500 named *rivers*, with the Mackenzie, running for 4,241 kilometres, being the longest. The Mackenzie ranks tenth in the world by length, thirteenth by drainage area, and fourteenth by average annual total discharge. Draining one-fifth of Canada, the Mackenzie River runs northwest beginning in Great Slave Lake, Northwest Territories, to the Beaufort Sea in the Arctic Ocean.

———————— ••• ————————

Rupert's Land comprised approximately one third of the Canadian land mass, encompassing all of the land containing waters draining into Hudson Bay (most of the Prairies and parts of Labrador, Nunavut, Northwest Territories, Ontario, and Quebec). In 1670, Charles II of England signed a charter giving the Hudson's Bay Company exclusive control over the area. It was named "Rupert's Land" for the King's cousin, who was the first governor of the Hudson's Bay Company. In 1870, the Canadian government purchased the land for $1.5 million—by land mass, Canada's largest-ever real estate deal.

———————— ••• ————————

The *rotary snowplow*, the *Robertson screw*, *AM radio*, and the *paint roller* are all Canadian inventions. In 1869, Dr. J. W. Elliott designed the first *rotary snowplow*, but he failed to attract investors to construct it. In later years, Orange Jull improved the design and the Elliott-Jull snowplow became a standard feature on trains in North America. *Peter Robertson* (1879–1951) patented his screw in 1907 and established a Canadian factory but failed to expand into England or the United States, which ultimately resulted in the inferior Phillips screw becoming the international standard in the Second World War. In 1906, Reginald Fessenden (1866–1932) developed amplitude modulation *(A.M.) radio*. His was the first long-distance public broadcast of music and voice. Fessenden lost his company in 1910, but in 1928 the US Radio Trust paid him $2.5 million for "contributions to radio technology."[27] Norman Breakey (1891–1965) invented the *paint roller* in the early 1940s but failed to patent it.

———————— ••• ————————

No. 9 for the Montréal Canadiens had won eight Stanley Cups and held almost twenty NHL records when he retired.

Maurice "Rocket" Richard (1921–2000) was extremely talented, fiercely competitive, and very short-tempered. In 1955, after a fight in which Richard struck a linesman, NHL president Clarence Campbell suspended him for the last three games of the regular season and all of the playoffs—a decision that prevented Richard from winning the scoring championship and perhaps the team from winning the Stanley Cup. There were riots in the streets of Montréal. For the French fans, the suspension seemed symbolic of every injustice ever experienced at the hands of the English. The riots awakened in English Canada a new awareness that the sleeping dragon of Quebec nationalism, if not fully awake, was certainly twitching its tail. When Richard retired from hockey, his number was raised to the rafters of the Montréal Forum and he was inducted into the Hockey Hall of Fame without the customary three-year waiting period. When he died, this Companion of the Order of Canada was given the first state funeral ever for a Canadian athlete.

— ••• —

Henri Richard (1936–2020), the younger brother of Maurice Richard, began his career as the "Pocket Rocket." A talented hockey player in his own right, he won eleven Stanley Cups (five in a row), which was more than any other player. When he retired, so did his sweater number: 16. Henri Richard was inducted into the Hockey Hall of Fame and the Canadian Sports Hall of Fame.

— ••• —

The *Richelieu River* (la Rivière Richelieu) was named for *Cardinal Richelieu*, the chief minister of King Louis XIII of France. In 1627, Cardinal Richelieu founded the privately financed Compagnie des Cent-Associés (Company of 100 Associates), which had the mandate to establish a French empire on the continent of North America by building French colonies of Roman Catholic settlers. The *Richelieu River* had great significance in the history of Quebec. It flows through the traditional lands of the Anishinaabe (Algonquin), Wendat (Huron), and Haudenosaunee (Iroquois) peoples. The fertile area was attractive to European settlers who started farms and used the river to transport goods. The government of New France deemed it to have strategic importance and built many forts along it.

S IS FOR SNOWBIRDS
    THAT SOAR THROUGH THE SKIES
AND ALSO FOR PEOPLE
    WHO FLEE WHEN SNOW FLIES

ST. LAWRENCE, SUZUKI,
    SECORD, SUNDANCE,
STORNOWAY, SASQUATCH,
    SASKATOONS, STAMPS

The official name for Canada's *Snowbirds* is 431 Air Demonstration Squadron of the Canadian Forces. They are part of a Canadian air show legacy that stretches back to 1919. One of the world's premier jet aerobatic teams, the Snowbirds were the first in the world to choreograph an airshow to music. They have performed at every major event in Canada and at every major air show in North America.

Non-military *snowbirds* are the people who fly south each winter to avoid the cold winter climate in Canada.

The dark-eyed junco, a ground-feeding bird that lives or breeds in every province and territory in Canada, is also called the *snowbird*.

— • • • —

Gene MacLellan's song "Snowbird" catapulted Canadian singer Anne Murray to an American gold record and international fame in 1970. The song was inducted into the Canadian Songwriters Hall of Fame in 2003.

The seasoned traveller, though not easily impressed, can readily recognize a spectacular sight when it appears. The Kanien'kehake "People of the Flint" (also referred to as Mohawk) called the river Kaniatarowanenneh, or the "big waterway." Jacques Cartier referred to it as the "rivière du Canada," and throughout the sixteenth century European explorers called it "The Great River." It was Cartier who christened it "*St. Lawrence.*" Cartier seemed to be in a naming kind of mood as he sailed into the estuary. Instead of asking his Indigenous hosts for the river's name, Cartier asked his ship's priest which saint's feast day was closest to the date of Cartier's arrival, and then, easily brushing aside a few thousand years of Indigenous history, he came up with "St. Lawrence River"—a catchy sort of name that has stood the test of time for half a millennium.

In geological terms, the St. Lawrence is a young river, formed ten thousand years ago when receding glaciers revealed a deep gash in the earth's crust. In Canadian historical terms, it is very old, the area having been inhabited by Indigenous peoples almost since its creation. Early European explorers of the St. Lawrence described a well-developed area with Indigenous

St. Lawrence River facts

* **Length:** 1,197 kilometres (the second longest in Canada after the Mackenzie River)

* **Width:** at its widest, over 100 kilometres

* **Depth:** at its deepest, 76.2 metres

* **Characteristics:** lakes, freshwater reaches, a long estuary, and a gulf with such marine features as a deep trench, high levels of salinity because the volume of ocean water at high tide exceeds the volume of fresh water at low tide, and the presence of marine species like seaweed and whales

* **Habitats:** deciduous, mixed, and coniferous forests and taiga

* **Fauna:** beluga whales, fish (herring, smelt, sturgeon), migratory birds, and before they were extirpated, walrus

* **Special status:** four Ramsar sites (under the 1971 Convention on Wetlands of International Importance, an international treaty for the conservation and wise use of wetlands), the largest of which is located in Lake Saint-Pierre (also a World Biosphere Reserve)

peoples hunting, fishing, and trading in canoes on the river, bark longhouses surrounded by palisades and gardens, and the well-established villages of Hochelaga (Montréal) and Stadacona (Quebec City) on its banks.

The St. Lawrence, which has an east-west orientation, is one of the few rivers that flow toward the centre of the continent; therefore the St. Lawrence River has made possible the development of Canada. During colonization, the river transported furs, trade goods, explorers, and settlers. By the mid-eighteenth century, most of the riverbank between Montréal and Quebec City was laid out in the long, narrow strips that characterize the French seigneurial system of farming. Because of the great river, Montréal and Quebec City became major commercial centres, and throughout the nineteenth century, the St. Lawrence was the main artery of the timber trade. The St. Lawrence remains Canada's most important commercial waterway today.

With its official opening on June 26, 1959, the St. Lawrence Seaway (a series of lakes, locks, canals, and channels) linked the Great Lakes and the St. Lawrence River to the Atlantic Ocean. With its opening, Canada became an exporter of iron ore. The construction of the Welland Canal (the western section of the Seaway) had an unforeseen effect on the environment because it allowed sea lamprey to bypass Niagara Falls and enter the rest of the Great Lakes. This caused the collapse of the lake trout population in Lake Superior.

Did You Know?

❋ The St. Lawrence hydrographic system (including the Great Lakes) covers a surface area of 1.6 million square kilometres (the third largest in North America after the Mississippi and the Mackenzie) and drains more than one-quarter of the earth's freshwater reserves.

❋ While exploring the St. Lawrence River in 1535, Jacques Cartier visited a fortified Indigenous village that he referred to as Hochelaga. The village had completely disappeared by the time Samuel de Champlain arrived in the early seventeenth century. To this date, no physical trace of Hochelaga has ever been uncovered.

MISSING:
The Haudenosaunee (Iroquoian) Village of Hochelaga

DESCRIPTION: Round in shape with approximately fifty bark-covered wooden houses; surrounded by palisades of three rows of wooden stakes fifteen metres high, driven deep into the earth; raised platforms piled with rocks and pebbles at the entrance and along the palisades. Last known location: cornfields close to Mount Royal in Montréal.

Last seen by Jacques Cartier, October 3, 1535.

REWARD: TBA; try contacting the Royal Canadian Geographical Society.

• • •

It is a long walk from a Japanese internment camp in Slocan City, British Columbia, to Rideau Hall in Ottawa. Along the way, *David Suzuki* (1936–) not merely passed but collected many milestones to become one of Canada's most well-known personalities and a Companion of the Order of Canada. He acquired a PhD in zoology and won academic acclaim as a geneticist and a professor at the University of British Columbia (where he is currently professor emeritus). A pioneer in promoting science literacy and in making science accessible to the general public, Suzuki became the first host of CBC Radio's popular science program *Quirks and Quarks*, and since 1979 has been the host of CBC's longest running television documentary series, *The Nature of Things with David Suzuki*. His 1985 series, *A Planet for the Taking*, attracted almost 2 million viewers per episode, shocked the Canadian public out of complacency into an uncomfortable awareness of the serious environmental issues facing Canada and the world, and was awarded the Environment Program medal from the United Nations. In 1990, he established the non-profit David Suzuki Foundation, which addresses environmental problems and solutions.

The recipient of numerous national and international awards, Suzuki has raised the ire of many businesspeople, industrialists, and politicians with his surprisingly controversial message that we should look after the environment upon which we all depend and his outspoken view that conventional economics is a form of "brain damage." Suzuki's honorary degree at the University of Alberta in 2018 was greeted with cheers for his environmental work and jeers for his assertion that Alberta's oil sands should be left in the ground to reduce carbon emissions.

Did You Know?

If you are Canadian, you have democratic rights, mobility rights, legal rights, equality rights, minority language educational rights, but you do *not* have the right to live in a healthy environment. The Blue Dot movement (a national campaign started by the David Suzuki Foundation and Ecojustice) advocates that Canadians be given that right in the Canadian *Charter of Rights and Freedoms*.

• • •

Although the actual historical record is somewhat unclear, *Laura Secord* (1775–1868) is celebrated as a hero of the War of 1812. She walked thirty kilometres from Queenston to Beaver Dams to warn the British garrison there of an imminent

American attack (which, as a result, was subsequently thwarted). A candy-maker from Toronto, Frank P. O'Connor, named his company after her because he considered her an icon of "courage, devotion, and loyalty."[28]

••••

The *Sundance* is a sacred midsummer celebration of the Plains Indigenous culture. The tradition embraces the circle as the symbol and the power of life and oneness (the sky, the earth, the moon, the planets, the seasons, and the life of a human all being circular), the connectedness of all things, and the sacredness of all things. The Sundance takes place in a circular enclosure with four gates (one for each of the four directions).

The Sundance has emotional, physical, and spiritual components. Participants prepare with blessings, prayers, a purification ritual in a Sweat Lodge, and four days of fasting with no food or water. During the four-day Sundance ceremony, they pierce their chests and dance under the hot sun (or other weather) for up to sixteen hours per day. Because the sun shines on everyone equally, the Sundance represents a fair and non-judgmental spiritual path. The piercings are a gift of flesh to the Creator. They are a physical manifestation of humbleness, of wisdom (the knowledge that the only thing that is truly ours is our body), of the embrasure of difficulties, and of sacrifice for others.

Traditionally an initiation rite for adolescent boys, the Sundance provided Indigenous peoples with an opportunity to form bonds, renew kinship ties, and trade. Between 1885 and 1951, the Sundance was banned under Canada's Indian Act. By 1960, the Sundance appeared to be dying as a tradition, but it has been undergoing revival since the latter decades of the twentieth century. Women and various age groups now participate, and the tradition has spread to the Elsipogtog First Nation of the Mi'kmaq in Nova Scotia. It is performed for individual and group healing, self-reflection, spiritual growth and reinforcement, and to engender pride in heritage and culture. The Sundance is sacred and cannot be photographed.

••••

Stornoway (named for a town on the Hebridean Isle of Lewis) is a spacious, classically designed, two-and-a-half–storey, stucco-clad "country house" located on wooded grounds at 541 Acacia Avenue in Ottawa's exclusive Rockcliff Park neighbourhood. The house was designed by well-known architect Allan Keefer and built in 1913 for Ascanio Joseph Major, a wealthy wholesale grocer. In 1923, ownership of the house passed to the Perley-Robertsons, who expanded it and named it Stornoway after the Perley ancestral home in Scotland. During the Second World War, Stornoway became the Ottawa residence of Crown Princess Juliana of the Netherlands. It has been the official residence of the federal Leader of the Opposition since 1950 and the property of the Government of Canada since 1970. Stornoway has housed many leaders of the opposition, including some who became prime minister, such as Jean Chrétien, Joe Clark, John Diefenbaker, Brian Mulroney, Lester Pearson, Pierre Trudeau, and John Turner. In 1993, Lucien Bouchard (leader of the Bloc Québécois) refused to live there, choosing instead to live across the river in Gatineau, Quebec. Stornoway is a Recognized Federal Heritage Building because of its architectural, environmental, and historical value.

· · ·

The word "*sasquatch*" comes from the Salish word "sasq'ets," which means "wild man" or "hairy man." Sasquatch is reportedly a large, ape-like creature with big footprints and superhuman speed and strength. It is certainly a legendary figure in Indigenous Traditional Stories, and less certainly a real creature living in the Squamish area of British Columbia. In Canada, sightings seem to happen after large quantities of beer have been drunk.

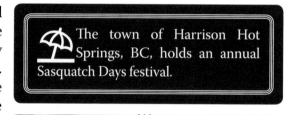
The town of Harrison Hot Springs, BC, holds an annual Sasquatch Days festival.

· · ·

Saskatoons (an anglicization of the Cree word "misâskwatômina," which means "berry fruit" or "fruit of the tree with many branches") are very hardy, cold-resistant, native plants that grow from western Ontario to British Columbia and the Yukon. The saskatoon plant are traditionally highly valued by Indigenous peoples, particularly the Siksika (Blackfoot) and the Nehiyawak (Cree), who often traded berries for other items. Indigenous people used every part of the plant. They fashioned arrow shafts from the hard, straight-grained wood and used the roots, inner bark, leaves, and berries to treat numerous minor ailments, including diarrhea, stomach problems, and snow blindness. The berries, which have high nutritional value, are a major ingredient in pemmican, and many non-Indigenous Canadians use them to make jams and pies. When saskatoon berries were first introduced to Britain in 2004, they were banned because they were incorrectly considered a genetically modified food that needed special testing. Later that year, Germany decided saskatoon berries were a regular food and declared them to be safe and healthy. Since 2014, saskatoon berries exported to some American states are called "juneberries" because researchers at Cornell University found that while Americans liked the taste, they did not like the name "saskatoon."

Saskatoon is also the name of the largest city in Saskatchewan.

——————— ••• ———————

Canada's *stamps* are very popular in philatelic circles because they are beautiful and because they reflect Canada's history and people. Here are more than enough facts to fit on the back of a postage stamp:

* CANADA'S FIRST STAMP: 1851. The Three-Pence Beaver, designed by Sir Sandford Fleming and issued with two other stamps—Six-Pence HRH Albert, the Prince Consort; Twelve-Pence Her Majesty Queen Victoria.

* FIRST FAMOUS STAMP ERROR: 1959. St. Lawrence Seaway inverted stamp. This stamp was the first significant mistake for Canada Post, which prided itself on preventing the accidental release of errors. An estimated four hundred exist, meaning that only eight error panes were released. Most are in private collections, but two have been placed in the National Archives of Canada.

* RAREST STAMP (PERHAPS): 1851. Twelve-Pence Black Queen Victoria (also called Twelve-Pence Black Stamp). Only 1,450 of these "Large Queen" stamps were sold during the three and a half years it was available; the rest were taken off the market and destroyed in 1857. Expensive in 1851, the stamp's value increased, fetching nearly $225,000 at a 2013 auction.

The first Black Canadian letter carrier was likely Albert Calvin Jackson (ca. 1856–1918), whose image is on the 2019 Black History Month stamp. He delivered mail for thirty-six years, from May 17, 1882, until his death in 1918. However, all was not smooth sailing. His hiring caused a tsunami of racist behavior. White postmen refused to train a Black man, so Jackson was reassigned as a hall porter. Newspapers raged on both sides, and the Black community protested to Prime Minister John A. Macdonald. Happily, it was an election year and Black votes counted. The tide turned and Albert Jackson was reinstated.

* **CANADA'S FIRST CHRISTMAS STAMP:** 1898. This stamp, which bears the inscription "XMAS 1898," was intended not to commemorate the Christian holiday, but rather to mark the inauguration of the Imperial Penny Postage rate (at the time, 2 cents). When Canadian Postmaster General William Mulock proposed that the stamp be issued on November 9 to "honour the Prince" (meaning the Prince of Wales), Queen Victoria was not amused and asked "What prince?" in a displeased manner. Mulock quickly replied, "Why, Madam, the Prince of Peace."

* **MOST FLAWED CHRISTMAS STAMP:** 1982. Thirty-Cent Christmas Fold-Over Stamp. The paper was unintentionally folded during the multi-colour process, causing a printing error that has increased the value of the stamp. One stamp was listed in the 2018 David Feldman catalogue at an estimated value of £5,000 to £10,000 GBP ($8,086 to $16,172 in Canadian dollars).

* **FIRST "PERMANENT" STAMP:** 2006. The permanent stamp, marked with a "P," can be used at any time regardless of a change in the domestic postage rate.

* **CANADA'S FIRST (UNOFFICIAL) POSTMEN:**

  * First Nations runners who carried messages between neighbouring bands using wampum beads. For Iroquoian runners, the colour of the wampum beads was a code for the type of message (white for messages of peace, prosperity, good will; blue for war, disaster, death).

  * Coureurs de bois and voyageurs carried messages during the fur trade.

* **CANADA'S FIRST (OFFICIAL) POSTMEN:**

* Pedro da Silva (1705) of Portugal, was appointed in New France to carry the governor's dispatches between Quebec, Montréal, and Trois Rivières.

* The Canada Post Office was established in 1867; letter carrier service was introduced in 1874.

Postmark: Some facts about Canada Post

* **Halifax, 1754:** Canada's first unofficial post office (established by stationer, Benjamin Leigh)

* **Halifax, 1755:** Canada's first official post office (established by Benjamin Franklin, Deputy Postmaster General of British North America)

* **Quebec, 1763:** Hugh Finlay becomes first Postmaster General at Quebec and establishes regular weekly service between Quebec and Montréal via Trois-Rivières

* **Champlain and St. Lawrence Railroad, ca. 1836:** The Champlain and St. Lawrence Railroad carries mail

* **Pre-Confederation Provinces, 1854:** installation of the first postal cars on trains; railway service continues to 1971

* **Pre-Confederation Provinces, 1859:** first parcel service

* **Canada, 1867:** establishment of the first national network of post offices

* **Canada, 1878:** Canada becomes a member of the international Universal Postal Union (to facilitate mail service between nations)

* **Canada, 1903:** unaddressed advertising and printed matter distribution services begin

* **Montréal to Toronto, 1918:** first airmail delivery (Captain Brian Peck)

* **Calgary to Edmonton, 1918:** Katherine Stinson delivers 259 authorized letters and becomes Canada's first woman airmail pilot

* **Canada, 1948:** Canada becomes the first country in the world to introduce domestic "all up" service (all mail is sent by air at the usual surface rate and no special air mail stickers are required)

* **Winnipeg, 1963:** installation of automated equipment to sort, stack, and cancel mail (first of its kind in North America)

* **Canada, 1981:** Canada Post Corporation is created as a Crown corporation.

T

T IS FOR TULIPS
    IN YELLOWS AND REDS
A THANK YOU FROM HOLLAND
    TO FILL FLOWER BEDS

TELEPHONE, TRUTH, TUQUE,
    TILLEY, AND TEEPEE
TOTEM POLES, TREES, TRAVOIS,
    TIMMY'S, TREATY

Since 1945, Canada has received an annual gift of *tulip* bulbs from Holland. The tulips express gratitude for Canada's role in liberating the country in the Second World War and for providing a place of refuge for members of the Royal Family during the war. The red and white Canada 150 tulip was the official tulip of Canada's sesquicentennial (150th anniversary) celebrations.

——————— ••• ———————

A Scottish immigrant to Canada, Alexander Graham Bell, invented the *telephone*. When speaking into the telephone for the first time, he famously said, "Mr. Watson, come here, I want you."[32]

——————— ••• ———————

After a faulty start in 2008, the *Truth and Reconciliation Commission of Canada (TRC)* was re-launched in 2009 with three newly appointed commissioners: Justice Murray Sinclair from the court of the Queen's Bench, Manitoba; lawyer Chief Wilton Littlechild from Maskwacis (Hobbema), Alberta; and CBC broadcaster Marie Wilson from Yellowknife, NWT. The TRC's mandate was to investigate the residential school system and to provide recommendations that would lead to a just and equitable future for Indigenous Canadians and a lasting reconciliation between Canada and Indigenous peoples.

The residential school system in Canada was a network of church-run, government-funded boarding schools for Indigenous children aged four to sixteen. This infamous system operated from the 1870s into the 1990s in all provinces and territories except New Brunswick, Newfoundland, and Prince Edward Island. The last residential school closed in 1996. When they existed, the schools had two mandates: to alienate Indigenous children from their families and their cultures (to "take the Indian out of the child"); and to assimilate them into the larger Euro-Canadian society. Attendance was mandatory and many young Indigenous children were forcibly removed from their homes and placed in the schools, where they were usually poorly educated, poorly fed, poorly looked after, greatly exploited (with the students supplying the labour for the schools), and greatly abused. The TRC's final report (released in 2015) stated that many of the approximately 150,000 Indigenous children who attended residential schools were sexually and physically abused and that approximately 3,200 (but likely many more) Indigenous children died in residential schools from tuberculosis, from other diseases caused by poor living conditions, and from malnourishment.

The report called on Canada to fully implement the 2007 United Nations Declaration on the Rights of Indigenous Peoples. Some of the rights enshrined in that document include the following: the right to self-determination and self-government; the right to preserve, maintain, and promote Indigenous cultural institutions; the right to be protected from assimilation or cultural genocide; the right to own and develop traditional lands and resources; the right to receive restitution or compensation for traditional lands; the right to protect the environment; the right to have treaties recognized, observed, and enforced; the right to experience improvements in social and economic situations; and the right to receive fair, just, and prompt resolution of conflicts.

The TRC's final report contains ninety-four specific recommendations. Among the list are calls for Canada to do the following: address the legacy of colonization of Canada's Indigenous peoples; abandon the Doctrine of Discovery; change the legal and policy frameworks that affect Indigenous people; conduct a national inquiry into missing and murdered Indigenous girls and women; provide more and better access to post-secondary education for Indigenous people; reduce the number of Indigenous foster children; provide more Indigenous programming on the CBC; and reduce the health-care gap between Indigenous people and other Canadians.

The government accepted the report's ninety-four recommendations. The National Inquiry into Missing and Murdered Indigenous Women and Girls officially began in 2016, and that commission released a final blistering report in 2019 that condemned Canadian society for indifference and inaction and for policies and institutions that perpetuate physical violence, that encourage human rights violations, and that constitute the genocide of Indigenous women, girls, two-spirit, lesbian, gay, bisexual, transgender, queer, questioning, intersex, and asexual people. The report called on Canada to decolonize, to reform the justice system, to improve the living conditions of Indigenous communities, and to introduce initiatives that empower Indigenous women and girls.

The *tuque* is a warm woollen cap worn in winter; the *Tilley hat* is the lightweight, long-lasting summer hat invented by Alex Tilley in 1980.

* * *

The Plains Indigenous peoples traditionally lived in *teepees*—cone-shaped dwellings with a smoke-hole at the top. Long poles were lashed together and covered with bison skins that were sometimes painted or decorated with quillwork.

* * *

Totem poles are vibrantly painted red cedar monuments created by Northwest Coast Indigenous peoples (Coast Salish, Haida, Kwakwaka'wakw, Nuxalt, Tlingit, Tsimshian) to symbolize ancestries, events, history, and people. The main types of totem poles include:

Did You Know?

* Totem pole carving reached its peak in the nineteenth century after European contact, when coastal First Nations people acquired metal tools and more wealth from fish and the fur trade.
* Charles Joseph carved a healing pole, a reminder of residential schools, that was erected in Montréal in 2017.
* The expression "low man on the totem pole" (meaning the person of the lowest rank or of the least importance) comes from a misunderstanding of the symbols on a totem pole. The figures on a totem

pole are not arranged in a hierarchical order; sometimes the lowest figure is the most important.

* Memorial poles, which can be erected to honour both the original owners and the new owners when a house changes hands; they can also commemorate the accomplishments or history of a member of a household who has died or a deceased chief or high-ranking individual.

* Mortuary poles, which serve a similar purpose; Haida mortuary poles include a place to store the remains or ashes of the person who has died.

* Grave markers, which are tombstones.

* Portal poles, which stand outside a house, depict a family lineage or history, and have a hole through which a person passes to enter a house.

* House poles, which might be decorated with family lineages; they stand inside to support the roof beams.

* Welcoming poles, which are frequently erected at potlatches and other ceremonies; they extend a warm welcome to important guests.

* Shaming or ridiculing poles, which are

Totem pole tidbits

* **COLOURS:** black, blue, blue-green, red, and sometimes white and yellow

* **HEIGHT:** usually three to eighteen metres (although they can be more than twenty metres)

* **ORIENTATION:** totem poles usually face the shore of an ocean or river

* **COMMONLY CARVED TOTEMS:** bear, beaver, eagle, frog, mosquito, orca, raven, salmon, shark, thunderbird (mythological), and wolf

* **LONGEVITY:** approximately sixty to seventy years (before decay)

* **FAMOUS CARVERS:** Charles Edenshaw (ca. 1839–1920), Henry Hunt (1923–1985), Richard Hunt (1951–), Stanley Hunt (1954–), Mungo Martin (1881–1962), Ellen Neel (1916–1966), Tim Paul (1950–)

less common than the other types of totem poles. They mock or criticize someone (a neighbour, or perhaps a government) for failing to act appropriately or with integrity. A shaming

From 1908 to 1912, **Emily Carr** travelled extensively along the British Columbia coast to document as accurately as possible totem poles in their original settings. While on site, she drew sketches and painted watercolours, which she later reworked as oil paintings. In 1927, the National Gallery of Canada included her work as part of an exhibit entitled *Canadian West Coast Art—Native and Modern*, which also included the works of Edwin Holgate, A. Y. Jackson, Langdon Kihn, and Ann Savage. It was here that Emily Carr was introduced to the Group of Seven and began a lifelong friendship with Lawren Harris.

pole might include inverted or distorted faces, upside-down figures, and/or body parts painted with colours that represent misdeeds. Traditionally, shaming poles are removed when the situation is rectified.

Today, both for Indigenous peoples and for Canadian society, totem poles represent the survival of First Nations in the face of cultural, political, and territorial infringement.

— ••• —

For Canadians, *trees* are a source of beauty and of revenue. The maple tree is Canada's official arboreal emblem, and its leaf is featured on the flag. Ten of the thirteen maple species native to North America grow in Canada, and at least one of each native species grows naturally in each Canadian province. Many maple leaves turn a vibrant red in the autumn. Sugar maples provide the sap for Canadian maple syrup. Lumberjacks, the loggers who felled trees and prepared timber for milling, have an important place in Canadian history, folklore, and arts. The job of lumberjack has been around for more than four hundred years. During the mid-1800s (the

Ti-Jean, child hero of French Canadian folklore, is a lumberjack capable of amazing feats. He might be the inspiration for Paul Bunyan, the legendary American lumberjack who also did amazing deeds.

🎼 *Lumberjack songs*

* "Canaday-I-O" (traditional)
* "The Log Driver's Waltz" (Wade Hemsworth)
* "The Lumber Camp Song" (traditional)
* "The Lumberjack Song" (Monty Python)

Many Canadian painters have been inspired by Canada's trees, including:

* Emily Carr
* S. M. Cosgrove
* The Group of Seven
* Tom Thomson

Lumberjacks lived in bush camps, worked from dawn to dusk six days per week, and burned seven thousand calories per day cutting trees by hand. (They ate a lot.) The work was dangerous, particularly for river drivers, who risked their lives on the logs in the rivers. Lumberjacks had a notorious reputation for partying and brawling when they returned from the woods in the spring

• • •

The Plains Indigenous peoples traditionally used a triangular frame of poles called a *travois* to transport baggage and teepee coverings. The frame looks much like a capital A with extra crossbars. Two long poles were tied together and harnessed at the top end to the shoulders of a dog or a horse, with the splayed ends dragging behind on the ground. The spaces between the splayed ends were joined with cross pieces to support baggage.

• • •

peak period for harvesting white pine), approximately 50 percent of Canadian males worked as lumberjacks.[31] Traditionally, the work was done in the winter when workers were available and when horses could draw the logs over the snow to the rivers.

The Tim Hortons chain of restaurants was started in the 1960s by NHL defenceman Tim Horton (1930–1974) and Hamilton policeman Ron Joyce (1930–2019). Originally known as Tim Horton's (with an apostrophe), the chain is said to have dropped the apostrophe after Quebec's Parti Québécois passed Bill 101—a language law making French the sole official language in Quebec and prohibiting businesses from posting signs in English. Because the apostrophe is an English punctuation mark, the restaurant chain dropped it. *Timmy's* is the "go-to" place in Canada for a double-double (a cup of coffee with two servings each of cream and sugar) and a doughnut. Participants in the annual RRRoll Up the Rim to Win promotion need not make a purchase first (you can get a free cup by writing to the contest address provided on the corporate website), and they have a one-in-six chance of winning a prize. The grand prize in the first RRRoll Up the Rim to Win in 1986 was a pack of Timbits; the 2019 grand prize was a Jeep Compass North. Canadian store Lee Valley Tools lists a Rimroller in its catalogue.

Tim Hortons customers span all age groups and genders and quite a few different species, with beavers, captured bears, goats, herds of deer, rescued moose, and rogue bulls making their appearance at various locations throughout Canada. Drive-thru customers have appeared on foot, on skates, on snowmobiles, in kayaks, on dog sleds, on a zamboni, and in a funeral procession.

At the request of Canadian Chief of Defence Staff General Rick Hillier (on behalf of troops deployed in Kandahar), Tim Hortons waived its usual franchise fees and opened an outlet at Kandahar Airfield in Afghanistan in 2006. Canadian Forces Personnel and Family Support Services operated the franchise, and the proceeds funded community and family programs for military families. During its five and a half years of operation, the Kandahar outlet served "four million cups of coffee, three million doughnuts, and half a million iced cappuccinos and bagels."[29] More than 230 Canadians travelled to Kandahar to work at Tim Hortons and to provide, in the words of employee Wendy Hayward, "five minutes of freedom from what they were doing, the heat, and the spiders, and the snakes."[30]

— ••• —

Indigenous *treaties* are recognized in the Canadian constitution as agreements between the government of Canada and Indigenous peoples. They are promises that, according to words spoken at the time, are to be kept "as long as the sun shines, the grass grows, and the rivers flow."[33]

The first treaties were alliances between Indigenous groups and either the British or the French, who were vying for control of Canada. The Peace and Friendship Treaties between the British and the Mi'kmaq and the Maliseet (1725–1779), were signed to secure Indigenous support for the English against the French.

Subsequent treaties described the exchange of traditional lands for certain promises and payments. After the British gained control of Canada, the British Royal Proclamation of 1763 stated that only the Crown could sign treaties with First Nations and only the Crown could purchase First Nation lands, and that only after the First Nation group had agreed to the sale at a public meeting of the group. The Upper Canada Treaties (1764–1862) and the Vancouver Island Treaties (1850–1854) were followed after Confederation by the Williams Treaties (1923) and the Numbered Treaties (Treaties 1 to 11).

Modern treaties can be comprehensive claims (settlements dealing with land claims not covered by treaties) or specific claims (which deal with specific grievances relating to the administration of First Nation lands and assets).

––––––––––––––– ••• –––––––––––––––

Treaties:
TWO OUTLOOKS

1. _No one forced Indigenous groups to sign treaties._

2. Indigenous groups had no choice. At the time the treaties were signed, their populations had been decimated by European diseases. The increase of European settlers and settlements had greatly diminished the wildlife (including the bison) that Indigenous peoples relied on for food, clothing, and shelter. Many groups were starving or facing imminent starvation. They therefore felt compelled to sign.

1. _Treaties were negotiated fairly._

2. Treaties were negotiated quickly, without adequate supports in place for the First Nations people. Most chiefs did not read English. They were given little, bad, or no advice and usually had to rely on translators (who were not always skilled or honest).

1. _Everyone is very clear about what was agreed to in the treaties._

2. There are many discrepancies between the oral and written versions of treaties. In 1996, the Supreme Court of Canada judged that treaties must be interpreted "in the sense that they would naturally have been understood by the Indians at the time of the signing."[34]

1. _Indigenous groups gave up their traditional lands in exchange for some benefits (reserves, annual or other payments, certain rights to hunting and fishing, ammunition, farm equipment and animals, educational and medical help)._

2. Indigenous groups did not give away their lands. Indigenous peoples point out that the surrender of land rights is based on the concept of private ownership of property, a concept that has never existed in First Nations custom or law. The oral versions of treaties contain no such transfer of property. They do contain protests about the loss of their land. Chief Poundmaker (Pîtikwahanapiwiyin) said, "This is our land, not a piece of pemmican to be cut off and given in little pieces. It is ours and we will take what we want."[35] For First Nations people, treaties are sacred covenants between autonomous peoples who agree to share the land and resources.

1. _First Nations surrendered their autonomy to the Canadian government._

2. First Nations people have never surrendered their autonomy, and they claim the right to self-government. The oral versions of treaties contain no such surrender; instead, they are agreements between two sovereign nations. First Nations people never agreed to assimilate or to give up their traditions.

1. _The treaties are beneficial for everyone._

2. The treaties as they have historically been interpreted are beneficial for Canadian governments because they give the Canadian government free rein to pursue agricultural settlement and resource development without the impediment of First Nations interests or involvement.

1. _Canadian governments have always fulfilled the obligations set out in the written treaties._

2. If that were so, there would be no current land claims or protests over misuse and abuse of natural resources. Residential schools would not have existed. First Nations people would not be living as disproportionately second-class citizens in a wealthy country.

U

U IS THE UMIAK,
   AN OPEN SKIN BOAT,
THOUGH HEAVILY LOADED
   IT STILL STAYS AFLOAT

UCLUELET, UAW,
   URANIUM, UNGAVA,
UNGER AND URSULINES,
   AND UPPER CANADA

The Inuit used the *umiak* in the summer for whaling or to transport people and goods to hunting grounds. Umiaks were usually constructed of driftwood and covered with skins from walruses or large bearded seals. They were wider and deeper than kayaks and could carry very heavy loads.

···

Many members of the *Ucluelet* (Nuu-chah-nulth) *First Nation* live in the traditional village of Hitacu (Ittattsoo), close to the town of *Ucluelet* (which in Nootka means "safe harbour" or "people of the sheltered bay") on the west coast of Vancouver Island, British Columbia. As a signatory of the Maa-nulth Treaty, the Ucluelet First Nation has had self-governance since 2011. Ucluelet has a safe landing harbour for canoes, but the area offshore is called the "Graveyard of the Pacific" because of the many shipwrecks. During the 1930s, Japanese settlers outnumbered all other groups in Ucluelet, and in the Second World War, Ucluelet unsuccessfully petitioned Victoria and Ottawa not to relocate the Japanese citizens farther inland.

Ucluelet is part of the Lighthouse Loop of the Wild Pacific Trail, and it also witnesses the spring migration of grey, humpback, and killer whales.

Did You Know?

Ucluelet holds the Canadian record for wettest day ever. On October 6, 1967, Ucluelet received 489 millimetres of rain.

···

The Canadian Region of the *UAW (United Automobile Workers)* was founded in 1937. It was later called the Canadian Auto Workers Union of Canada. In 2013, it became Unifor after merging with the Communications, Energy, and Paperworkers Union of Canada (CEP) to form one of the largest unions in the country. The UAW was responsible for the 1937 Oshawa Strike, which had a significant influence on labour relations in Canada. Four thousand workers at the General Motors plant in Oshawa, Ontario, went on strike for two weeks, demanding an eight-hour day, higher wages, improved working conditions, and recognition of the union. General Motors management, aided by Mitchell Hepburn, then Premier of Ontario, fought the union with Hepburn's special police force (dubbed "Hepburn's Hussars" or "Sons-of-Mitches"), but the UAW won the first major victory for Canadian unionized workers.

The UAW is also the force behind the Rand Formula, a labour law that resulted from the 1946 UAW strike at the Ford plant in Windsor, Ontario. Because of this law, workers who are included under collective bargaining contracts must pay union dues even if they are not union members. The formula also stipulates that the union and its members can face sanctions if they participate in illegal work stoppages. The Rand Formula gives workers the freedom to choose or reject union membership, and it prevents non-union members from getting a free ride when unions achieve gains for workers. The Rand Formula also gives unions financial security, which ensures their long-term survival, and places on them the responsibility to act within the law.

———————— ••• ————————

Canada is one of the world's largest producers of *uranium*, most of which is mined in northern Saskatchewan. Uranium is a heavy metal with several different isotopes. Uranium-235 splits easily, giving off enormous amounts of energy and heat—a characteristic that has made the element increasingly important throughout the world as a source of electricity and power. Almost all of the uranium mined in Canada is exported, with a small percentage being used in CANDU reactors in Canada. (Although Canada's nuclear sector provides tens of thousands of jobs and contributes billions of dollars annually to Canada's economy, this industry is controversial because two problematic by-products are radioactive waste and nuclear bombs.)

It is against Canadian law to sell uranium to anyone who plans to use it to build nuclear weapons or nuclear explosive devices. In 1974, after India exploded an atomic bomb made with Canadian uranium, Canada became a founding member of the Nuclear Suppliers Group, which aims to uphold the Nuclear Non-Proliferation Treaty and to ensure that non-military nuclear trade does not advance the spread of nuclear weaponry.

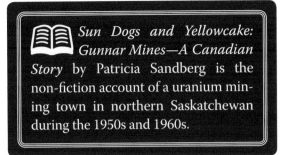

Sun Dogs and Yellowcake: Gunnar Mines—A Canadian Story by Patricia Sandberg is the non-fiction account of a uranium mining town in northern Saskatchewan during the 1950s and 1960s.

•••

The waves of Hudson Bay, Hudson Strait, and *Ungava Bay* wet the waterfront of Quebec's *Ungava Peninsula*. Possible translations of the Inuktitut word "ungava" include "toward open water," "far away," "unknown land," and "place visited by white whales." The Inuit have traditionally occupied the coastal areas of the peninsula, which is also home to two migratory caribou herds. Part of the Canadian Shield, Ungava Peninsula is covered with lakes, minerals, and permafrost. The area experiences some of the coldest winters in Canada. Ungava Peninsula is also the site of several impact craters. The youngest of these, at only 1.4 million years, is the Pingualuit (or Nouveau-Québec) Crater. The lake that occupies the crater is world-renowned for its exceedingly clear, cobalt-coloured water. Soil analysis at the crater has revealed that the meteorite was a chondrite, probably originating in the asteroid belt between Mars and Jupiter. A true "smash hit," the impact is estimated to have released 8,500 times the energy of the atomic bomb that devastated Hiroshima in the Second World War.

•••

Jim Unger (1937–2012) was a world-famous cartoonist who created the comic strip *Herman*. In the early 1970s, Unger was hired by the *Mississauga Times* to do editorial cartoons and advertising art. His editor, Phil Bingley, recognized Unger's talent and felt he deserved a wider audience, but Canadian syndicates and newspapers turned down Unger's work. In 1974, Unger sent some work to Universal Press Syndicate in Kansas City, and they sent a ten-year contract by return mail. Unger is considered a trailblazer in single-panel, offbeat humour. Much admired by the public and his peers, he was a two-time winner of the National Cartoonists Society's Newspaper Panel Cartoon Award.

•••

The *Ursulines* arrived in Canada in the early part of the seventeenth century to answer a call for religious women to educate and convert Indian girls to Christianity. Madame de la Peltrie, a French widow, arrived in Quebec in 1639, accompanied by three Augustinian nuns, who founded the Hôtel-Dieu (the first hospital north of Mexico), and three Ursuline nuns, who founded the Ursuline Seminary of New France (the first educational institution in North America). Mother Marie de l'Incarnation translated dictionaries, grammars, and books on Christian doctrine into the Wendat, Algonkin, Montagnais, and Iroquois languages. These resources were used in subsequent centuries by missionaries throughout Canada.

The first students of the seminary were Indigenous girls, followed by daughters of French colonists and, later, Irish Catholics. Students were taught arts and sciences. Many branches of the original convent spread across North America. Ursuline convent schools housed Canada's first normal school for training teachers and Canada's first school of domestic science.

The Ursuline Monastery is a National Historic Site. Visitors can see where Ursuline sisters nursed the wounded soldiers of Wolfe and where the remains of Louis-Joseph de Montcalm were initially buried before being moved to the crypt of the Hôpital-Général de Québec.

Did You Know?

Because of the Ursulines, in Canada's early years, girls were better educated than boys.

* * *

Upper Canada was created in 1791, when the colony of Quebec was divided into two regions. The eastern region became Lower Canada (now the province of Quebec), and the western region became Upper Canada (now the province of Ontario). Upper Canada was originally inhabited by First Nations peoples (Algonquin, Huron-Wendat, Neutral, Tionontatehronnon (Petun), French settlers and missionaries, and later by American Loyalists and

* Until 1763: New France
* After 1763: Province of Quebec (Quebec, Ontario, and part of the United States)
* 1791–1841: Upper Canada
* 1841–1867: Canada West
* 1867–present: Ontario

land-needy farmers. After the War of 1812, Britons settled in Upper Canada. The first Lieutenant-Governor, John Graves Simcoe, feared an excess of democracy and, in imitation of British society, he tried to recreate in Upper Canada an aristocratic governing class. To that end, he cemented ties with the Anglican clergy and with a small group of like-minded elites, who were later given the derogatory name "Family Compact" by reformers. The members of the Family Compact maintained strong business, family, political, and religious ties with each other. They answered only to the lieutenant-governor (and not to the legislative assembly), and they actively opposed democratic reform and the idea of responsible government. The Family Compact promoted loyalism to Britain, the Anglican church, and to themselves. The subsequent 1837 rebellions against British rule in both Upper Canada and Lower Canada led to the Durham Report (1839), the union of the two entities of Upper and Lower Canada into the Province of Canada (1841), and the granting of responsible government.

Sainte-Marie Among the Hurons has been recreated on its original site in Midland, Ontario. Martyrs' Shrine (the only National Shrine outside of Quebec), built to honour the lives of St. Jean de Brebeuf and his companions, is also located in Midland.

V

V IS FOR VINLAND,
    THE LAND OF THE VIKING,
WHO APPARENTLY DIDN'T FIND MUCH
    TO HIS LIKING

VANIER, VICTORIA,
    VANCOUVER, VOYAGEUR,
VIMY RIDGE, VICTORY BONDS,
    VOLES, DE VERCHÈRES

Around 1000 CE, the Vikings, led by Leif the Lucky, settled for a short time on the east coast of North America. They had a base camp in Vinland (Land of the Vine), so named by Leif Eriksson when he discovered wild grapes growing in the area. The exact location of *Vinland* is unknown, but might be in New Brunswick, where wild grapes grow. L'Anse aux Meadows in Newfoundland is an archaeological site containing the remains of a Viking settlement.

• • •

The road of unity is the road of love: love of one's country and faith in its future will give new direction and purpose to our lives, lift us above our domestic quarrels, and unite us in dedication to the common good.... I pray God that we may all go forward hand in hand. We can't run the risk of this great country falling into pieces.[36]

-Georges-Philéas Vanier

Georges-Philéas Vanier (1888–1967) was the Governor General of Canada from 1959 to 1967. Vanier was the first French Canadian appointed to the position, and his appointment began the tradition of alternating between English- and French-speaking governors general. Although Vanier was very popular with most factions of the Canadian public, some Quebec separatists considered him a traitor to the Quebec people.

• • •

The site of *Victoria*, the capital city of British Columbia, has been inhabited by humans for more than four thousand years. Named for Queen Victoria of England, the city is located on traditional lands of the Coast Salish Indigenous peoples. Many British and Chinese and Hispanic people arrived in Victoria with the Fraser Gold Rush of 1858. Victoria has the oldest Chinatown in Canada, and its Fan Tan Alley is Canada's narrowest commercial street (0.9 metres wide at the narrowest section). Fan Tan Alley is named for a gambling game and was the site of opium factories until 1908, when the factories were closed because opium production became illegal in Canada.

hosted the world's fair (Expo 86) and the 2010 Olympic Games.

In 2014, Vancouver City Council unanimously voted to acknowledge that the city is situated on Indigenous lands that were never ceded to a Canadian government. The council also declared 2014 the Year of Reconciliation—a real attempt at addressing existing issues between First Nations and the City of Vancouver. At the end of the year, Vancouver City Council participated in a once-banned sacred First Nation ceremony to "brush off" with cedar boughs any negative and troubling issues that could impede clear thinking and obstruct cooperation.

> Visitors to Victoria can experience a traditional English afternoon tea at The Fairmont Empress, which serves 500,000 cups of tea each year.

Did You Know?

In 1866, Mifflin Gibbs (1823–1915) became Canada's first Black politician and the first Black person elected to public office in British Columbia when he won a seat on Victoria City Council.

⋯

Vancouver, named for Captain George Vancouver, is the largest city in British Columbia. Its location has been home to the Coast Salish people for thousands of years. The Spanish were the first Europeans to arrive, but they stayed just long enough to leave behind a few street names. They were followed by Captain Vancouver, Simon Fraser, the Hudson's Bay Company, prospectors in the Fraser Gold Rush, and many other immigrants. Vancouver is North America's second largest port after New York, but Stanley Park is bigger than Central Park. Vancouver has

Did You Know?

Vancouver's Gastown takes its name from a chatty fellow called "Gassy Jack," who opened a tavern for forestry workers in 1867; a community (Gastown) grew up around the saloon.

⋯

Voyageurs were licensed workers, minor partners, or free contractors in Canada's fur trade. They replaced the coureurs de bois. Voyageurs transported goods (usually by canoe) to trading posts.

"Porkeater" (*mangeur de lard*) was initially a disparaging term for the North West Company voyageurs who only travelled between Montréal and Grand Portage. A porkeater's diet was mainly pork (as opposed to the "real" voyageur diet of fish and pemmican). Later, the term "porkeater" meant any rookie voyageur. Each voyageur probably ate about five thousand calories per day. Voyageurs were not usually taller than five foot six because there was not much room in a canoe for long legs. They were very muscular and strong as they needed to paddle about thirty thousand strokes per day. They could travel 130 kilometres on a given day if conditions were good. Each man also had to be able to carry six pieces (of furs, supplies, merchandise) on portages. Each piece weighed ninety pounds, and the voyageur usually carried two at once.

Canadian artists inspired by voyageurs include Frances Anne Hopkins and Paul Kane.

Voyageurs sang as they paddled, and good singers got extra pay. Voyageur songs were internationally known and loved. "Alouette" and "En roulant ma boule" are voyageur songs.

At the end of the battle at *Vimy Ridge* in the First World War, Canadian Brigadier-General A. E. Ross famously said, "In those few minutes, I witnessed the birth of a nation."[37] He also witnessed the death or injury of more than ten thousand men. After both the English and the French tried unsuccessfully to wrest control of the ridge from the Germans, the Canadians were assigned the "impossible" task. For the first time, all four Canadian divisions fought together, and together they secured the victory that changed the course of the war. Four Canadians (Private William Johnstone Milne of the 16th Battalion, Captain Thain Wendell MacDowell of the 38th Battalion, Private John George Pattison of the 50th Battalion, and Lance-Sergeant Ellis Wellwood Sifton of the 18th Battalion) were awarded the Victoria Cross—the highest military honour in the British Empire. Of the recipients, only Captain MacDowell survived. Vimy Ridge was a defining moment in the evolution of a national Canadian identity because, for the first time, individuals from across Canada worked together and sacrificed for the collective good of the country. Vimy Ridge also marked the change in Canada's status from British colony to independent member of the Commonwealth. Because of Vimy Ridge, Canada had a separate signature on the Treaty of Versailles, the treaty that ended the First World War.

— ••• —

"Yours not to do and die—Yours but to go and buy *Victory Bonds* 1918" was one of the slogans on posters advertising the sale of Victory Bonds during the First World War. The Canadian government sold these bonds during both world wars to Canadian individuals, corporations, and other organizations to raise funds to pay for the war effort.

— ••• —

Voles are often called field mice. They look like mice but have shorter tails, rounded snouts and heads, and small ears. In Canada they live in a variety of biomes— low arctic tundra, taiga, aspen parkland, grasslands, boreal forests. Voles are active during the day and night, and they feed on green plants and seeds. During the winter, they travel through snow-covered tunnels. They do not usually survive more than one winter.

— ••• —

Madeleine de Verchères (1678–1747) became a Canadian heroine when in 1692, at age fourteen, she defended her family's fort from Iroquois invaders. Accounts vary, but the gist of the story is that Madeleine's parents were away, leaving two cowardly soldiers, an eighty-year-old man, Madeleine, and her two younger brothers alone in the fort. Madeleine was outside the fort when an Iroquois war party attacked and captured several people. Some warriors chased Madeleine to the gate of the fort. Madeleine evaded capture by the fleet-footed Iroquois, closed the gate, pretended the fort was full of soldiers, and fired off a cannon with the dual purpose of scaring off the invaders and warning other nearby forts of danger. Madeleine and her small band held off the invaders for another eight days. During that trying time, some French visitors arrived by canoe. Madeleine bravely went out to meet them and to escort them safely into the fort. Madeleine reasoned that the Iroquois would think that she would never dare to leave the fort unless she was well-protected. They would believe that she was merely a decoy sent out to lure them to the fort, where they would be massacred by large numbers of soldiers waiting to ambush them. Whatever they might have thought, the Iroquois did not attack Madeleine, and she and her small party safely entered the fort and continued to defend it until outside help arrived.

The Madeleine de Verchères National Historic Site of Canada is located in Verchères, Quebec.

W

W IS WATER
    AND WONDERFUL WHEAT
WITH EACH IN ABUNDANCE
    TO DRINK AND TO EAT

WINNIPEG, WAMPUM,
    WIGWAMS, AND WAPITI,
WOLVERINES, WAR BRIDES,
    WALRUS, WHALES, WINNIE

Canada is surrounded by three oceans— the Pacific, the Arctic, and the Atlantic— and its coastline stretches for more than 243,000 kilometres. Lakes and rivers cover about 12 percent of Canada's surface area, with most of it draining north into the Arctic Ocean or Hudson Bay. Ontario alone has more than 250,000 lakes—about 20 percent of the entire world's fresh *water* supply.

———— ••• ————

Wheat has been grown in Canada since the early 1600s. Approximately half of the wheat grown in Canada comes from Alberta, Saskatchewan, and Manitoba, the provinces known as "Canada's breadbasket." In 1911, Marquis wheat won $1,000 in gold from the Canadian Pacific Railway for being the best wheat variety in Canada. Its developer, Dr. Charles Saunders, invented a "chewing test" in which he would chew the kernels from several heads of wheat to determine which had the greatest elasticity and hence would make the largest loaves of bread. All Canadian wheat varieties developed in the past one hundred years derive from crosses with Marquis wheat.

———— ••• ————

Winnipeg (derived from the Cree word "win-nipi," meaning murky water) is both the capital and the largest city of Manitoba. Situated at the confluence of the Red and Assiniboine Rivers, Winnipeg is known as the "Gateway to the West"; however, the "Golden Boy" at the top of the dome on the legislature building faces north. This is because the decision-makers in 1919 assumed that Manitoba's future expansion and prosperity would come from the northern part of the province.

Did You Know?

All Canadian coins for circulation are produced at the Winnipeg branch of the Royal Canadian Mint.

WHICH OF THE FOLLOWING ARE NICKNAMES FOR WINNIPEG?

A. Chicago of the North
B. Slurpee Capital of the World
C. Winterpeg

ANSWER: All of the above.

Wampum (a Narragansett word meaning "string of white shell beads") are tubular white and purple beads traditionally made on the East Coast from whelk shells (white) and quahog clam shells (purple). Indigenous peoples traditionally used wampum in ceremonies, for diplomacy, and as trade currency and ornaments. They are a particularly important part of the oral history record, and they symbolize respect and peace and mutual agreement between groups. Wampum belts were sometimes used to validate treaties with Europeans.

Traditional dwellings of the Algonquin peoples of eastern Canada were called *wigwams*. They are domed or conical in shape and were usually covered with bark or reed mats. Like teepees, wigwams are portable. It was traditionally women's work to take down and set up wigwams.

The word "*wapiti*" is Shawnee for "white rump," and it refers to members of the deer family that are often called American elk. They are also called "waskasoo" (Nehiyawak/Cree) and "ponoka" (Siksika/Blackfoot). Wapiti graze and browse in the Rockies and on Vancouver Island. Second in size to the moose, wapiti are integral to the Banff National Park ecosystem because they are the chief herbivores and an important food source for wolves.

Wapiti are the most vocal members of the deer family. Cows and calves squeal and chirp at each other. Members of a herd call to warn of danger or simply to announce their presence to others. In the fall, the bulls advertise their fitness and general excellence by bugling. Strong bugle calls can attract willing cows to a bull's harem, or they can attract male competitors wanting to challenge the bugler.

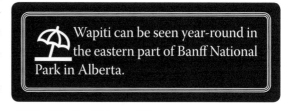

Wapiti can be seen year-round in the eastern part of Banff National Park in Alberta.

The healthy respect that the *wolverine* is given for its ferocity and survival skills is not overly obvious in the names it is called by humans. Its scientific name *Gulo gulo* means "glutton." Wolverines are also simply called gluttons, stink bears, or skunk bears. In Indigenous Traditional Stories, wolverines are usually bullies or anti-social tricksters. These fierce, solitary, nocturnal animals are the largest of the weasel family and live primarily in British Columbia and the North. A male wolverine's scent marks his territory, which he will only share with females. The wolverine is well adapted to snowy conditions because of its dense fur, its crampon-like claws, and because its paws have built-in snowshoes; when it takes a step, its paw almost doubles in size as it touches the ground. Wolverines use snow for dens and as refrigerators for storing food. Wolverines are sneaky and fierce. They can smell and kill prey that is hibernating under twenty feet of snow. They are omnivorous and not particularly fussy about their food, although they much prefer meat to other foods. They will dine on fresh or dead prey, and they devour bones and teeth as well as meat. Indigenous peoples traditionally preferred wolverine hair for parka hoods because the outer hairs shed frost without it melting. Global warming is a threat to the existence of wolverines.

The *war brides* were (mostly British) women who married Canadian servicemen overseas and then immigrated to Canada during and after the Second World War. The first marriage of a Canadian soldier to an English woman occurred less than two months after the first troops arrived in

Why life in Canada was often difficult for war brides

* Many had married hastily and did not know their husbands very well.

* Many husbands were injured and/ or traumatized by the war and were no longer the dashing, carefree young men the war brides had married.

* Many war brides were city girls and had to adapt to rural life without conveniences like indoor toilets and running water.

* War brides usually had no friends or family (apart from those of their husbands). Upon arrival in Canada, if a husband could not meet his war bride, volunteers welcomed her and either accompanied her or arranged for her safe transport to her husband.

England in 1939. By the spring of 1948, the Canadian government had provided free sea and rail transport to Canada for nearly seventy thousand women and children.

———————— ••• ————————

The Atlantic *walrus* inhabits Hudson Bay and the coast of Labrador in the Atlantic Ocean. Walruses divide themselves by gender into all-male and all-female herds. They use their ivory tusks (canines that can be one metre long) to break up ice, to climb out of the water, to establish dominance, and for defence. Walruses are non-aggressive carnivores that mainly eat shellfish. Traditionally, the Inuit hunted the walrus primarily for ivory and dog meat. The Northwest Atlantic walrus population has been extirpated.

———————— ••• ————————

More than thirty species of *whales* swim in Canada's waters. Though the country banned commercial whaling in 1972, centuries of the practice significantly reduced whale numbers in Canada.

Whale watching is now a popular pastime. On the East Coast, watchers can look for the North Atlantic right whale—a baleen-plated whale that can eat more than 2,500 kilograms of food each day. Known for their callosities (raised patches of roughened skin that scientists use as identity markers), they are slow swimmers but can hold their breath underwater for up to forty minutes. Watchers have seen them breaching, lobtailing, and flippering.

In Arctic waters or in the St. Lawrence River, observers might hope to hear the many vocalizations of the extremely social beluga, which is nicknamed the "sea canary." White in colour, belugas are easily identified by the melon on their heads, which they use for orientation and echolocation of prey.

Whale watching in Canada

- **British Columbia**: grey, humpback, minke, orca

- **Quebec**: beluga, humpback, minke

- **New Brunswick**: finback, humpback, minke, North Atlantic right, sei

- **Nova Scotia**: finback, humpback, minke, North Atlantic right, pilot

- **Newfoundland & Labrador**: beluga, blue, fin, humpback, minke, pilot, sperm

Whale watchers on the West Coast can easily recognize the tall dorsal fin of the black and white orca (or killer) whale. These highly social whales live in family groups called matrilines (usually headed by a family's oldest female plus her offspring and her daughters' offspring). They use echolocation to locate prey and often hunt in packs for chinook and chum salmon.

As magnificent as these creatures are, they are no match for humans. Our pollution, our human-induced climate change, our habitat destruction, and our excessive ship traffic are relentlessly driving whale species to extinction.

Did You Know?

* The North Atlantic right whale population, the beluga's St. Lawrence estuary population, and the orca's Northeast Pacific northern resident population all have a SARA (Species at Risk Act) status of "endangered." Sixteen other species are currently listed as extirpated, endangered, threatened, or of special concern.
* It doesn't always pay to be right. The right whale was so named by whalers, who considered it the "right" whale to kill because it is a slow swimmer, it is often found close to shore, it provides enormous quantities of blubber and oil, and it floats when it is dead.

• • •

The inspiration for the children's story *Winnie-the-Pooh* (by A. A. Milne) was a Canadian bear cub named *Winnie*. In 1914, while en route to join the Canadian troops at Valcartier, Quebec, veterinarian Lieutenant Harry Colebourne purchased an orphaned black bear cub from a trapper at White River, Ontario. He named the bear "Winnipeg" after his Canadian hometown, and the bear became the mascot of the Fort Garry Horse Regiment of the 3rd Canadian Division. Winnie travelled to England with the regiment, but when the regiment was sent to France, Colebourne lent the cub to the London Zoo, where author A. A. Milne and his son, Christopher Robin, were among the bear's many frequent visitors.

• • •

X IS CAMP X
	DURING WORLD WAR TWO,
SECRETS AND SPIES
	WERE SURE TO PASS THROUGH

XELAS AND XENA
	(A GOD AND A TOWN),
THE XY COMPANY
	(OF MODEST RENOWN)

Camp X was a radio communications centre and training school for secret agents during the Second World War—the first facility of its kind in North America. A joint British, Canadian, and American project, it was started by Sir William Stephenson (also called "Intrepid") and located near Whitby, Ontario. It recruited Canadians, Americans, and new North American immigrants with insider knowledge of European languages and cultures. Camp X provided preliminary training only; suitable candidates furthered their training in England and were then sent behind enemy lines as spies and saboteurs. Ian Fleming, creator of James Bond, is said to have been a recruit of Camp X.

Camp X buildings were demolished in 1969 and bulldozed into Lake Ontario. Relics routinely wash up on the beach. A walk on the shoreline provides an opportunity to see many artifacts from Camp X. A cleanup of Lake Ontario would provide an opportunity to see many more.

• • •

In Northwest Coast Traditional Stories, *Xelas* is a "transformer god" who transforms dirt into human beings. The concept of "transformer" originates with the Salish peoples; in their Traditional Stories, transformer figures can change humans into animals (or vice versa); alter landscapes; render monsters inanimate; and reduce monsters to ordinary beings. In some Indigenous traditions, such trickster characters as Coyote and Raven are also transformers.

• • •

Xena is a Saskatchewan ghost town, the last of its buildings having been demolished in the 1970s. It was part of the Canadian National Railway's alphabet system for naming sidings across the Prairies and fell between Watrous and Young.

• • •

The *XY Company* came into existence as the New North West Company in the late 1790s. It was called the XY Company because it marked its bales with "XY" to set them apart from the bales of the North West Company. The two companies merged in the early 1800s. The XY Company was a direct competitor to the Hudson's Bay Company in the fur trade.

• • •

Y

Y IS THE YORK BOAT
    THAT PLIED THE NORTHWEST
SPORTING THE HUDSON'S BAY
    COMPANY'S CREST

YELLOWHEAD, YUKON,
    YORKTON, AND YOHO,
YELLOWKNIFE, YOUNG,
    AND YUKON POTATO

The Hudson's Bay Company used *York boats* for inland travel in the Canadian northwest. More stable and hardy than canoes, they carried the same number of crewmen but double the cargo. They were also equipped with sails for lake travel.

———— ••• ————

William Yellowhead (Musquakie) (d. 1864) was an Anishinaabe chief who fought for Canada in the War of 1812. He also held the wampum belt signifying lasting peace between the Anishinaabe and the Haudenosaunee (Iroquois). Along with other Anishinaabe Chiefs, Musquakie surrendered to the British government traditional lands in the present-day Grey, Wellington, Dufferin, and Simcoe counties of Ontario. The Muskoka region of Ontario likely takes its name from him.

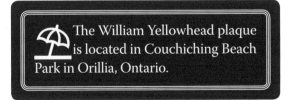
The William Yellowhead plaque is located in Couchiching Beach Park in Orillia, Ontario.

———— ••• ————

The *Yellowhead Pass* crosses the continental divide between Alberta and British Columbia. This route, which had long been traversed by Indigenous peoples and later by fur traders transporting mainly moose or caribou hides, was originally called Leather Pass. It was renamed for "Tête Jaune," a blond Metis trapper by the name of Pierre Bostonais, who led one of the first survey expeditions through the pass. Because of its low elevation (1,133 metres), Sandford Fleming recommended the Yellowhead Pass for the CPR route through the mountains, but this recommendation was overruled in favour of the Kicking Horse Pass farther south. In 1942, interned Japanese Canadians worked on a roadway through the Yellowhead Pass, but it was not until the late 1960s that motorists could drive on paved roads all the way from Jasper to Vancouver. A highway, a railway, a pipeline, and a fibre-optics route all currently traverse the Yellowhead Pass.

———— ••• ————

The word "*Yukon*" comes from the Gwich'in word for the Yukon River, "Yu-kun-ah," which means "great river." The Yukon River flows partly in the United States. It is the tenth longest river in Canada and one of the longest rivers in the world. The Yukon River is of historical importance to First Nations people and was extensively used by prospectors in the Klondike Gold Rush. Until the Klondike Highway was completed in the 1950s, people travelled by paddlewheel riverboats on the Yukon River. The narrow and scenic Thirty Mile Section has caused more shipwrecks than any other section of the river.

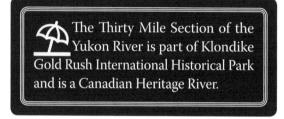

The Thirty Mile Section of the Yukon River is part of Klondike Gold Rush International Historical Park and is a Canadian Heritage River.

• • •

Since their discovery in 1997, the *Yukon Ice Patches* have spawned a new branch of research—ice patch archaeology. The ice patches are accumulations of winter snow and ice that do not melt away in summer. Unlike glaciers, they do not move (apart from some seasonal melting around the edges). The oldest Yukon ice patches contain ice and artifacts (usually hunting tools) that are more than nine thousand years old. Because they were encased in ice, many artifacts are extremely well preserved. Many of the objects are organic in nature and can be reliably dated using radiocarbon technology. First Nations people are actively involved in Yukon Ice Patch archaeology and research.

Some discoveries include:

* a 1,400-year-old moccasin (the oldest known in Canada)

* a willow dart shaft that is nearly 5,000 years old

* throwing boards and hunting darts that are at least 9,000 years old

* well preserved bows and arrows from around 1,200 years ago

* bison remains that are 300 to 10,000 years old

* painted objects, sinews, hides, feathers.

• • •

In 1882, at the invitation of the York Farmers' Colonization Company (a group of Toronto businessmen), an assortment of settlers from York County, Ontario, plus other pioneers from the Maritimes, Quebec, Great Britain, and the United States, established York Colony in Saskatchewan. The York Farmers' Colonization Company had purchased the land from the Dominion Government, which was selling charters to various companies as part of its Western expansion initiative. Such charters allowed the participating companies to undertake all of the activities necessary for founding a settlement. The companies could buy and sell land, establish businesses, operate ferry services, construct roads, and act as government homesteading agents. In 1884, with the opening of the post office, the name of the hamlet changed from York Colony to *Yorkton*, and in 1890, when the railroad arrived, Yorkton moved to its present location. At the beginning of the twentieth century, the railway and the promise of land brought immigrants, many initially from the Ukraine, Russia, Germany, and the United States. Later immigrants have come from all over the world.

•••

The name for *Yoho National Park* comes from a Cree utterance that signifies awe or wonder. Situated in the southeastern corner of British Columbia, the park shares borders with Banff National Park, Kootenay National Park, and Hamber Provincial Park. Non-Indigenous people first came across Yoho during the CPR search for a suitable pass through the mountains. Camp Otter, a First World War prisoner-of-war camp, was located in Yoho from 1915 to 1916. The government being rather tight-fisted with park funding, it was the prisoners who built a highway and a bridge for nothing (not counting free room and board). A land of majestic mountains, tumbling waterfalls, turquoise lakes, rushing rivers, and Burgess Shale fossils, Yoho National Park is home to numerous wildlife including moose, wolverines, wapiti, and grizzlies.

Yoho National Park is one of seven parks that make up the Canadian Rocky Mountain Parks UNESCO World Heritage Site. The other six parks are: Banff National Park, Jasper National Park, Kootenay National Park, Hamber Provincial Park, Mount Assiniboine Provincial Park, and Mount Robson Provincial Park.

Yoho National Park has three national historic sites: Abbot Pass Refuge Cabin, Kicking Horse Pass, and Twin Falls Tea House.

•••

Yellowknife is the capital—and only—city of the Northwest Territories. It is named for the Yellowknives, a Dene band who were in turn named for the copper knives they carried. The first non-Indigenous person to arrive was probably Peter Pond, a fur trader with the North West Company. Gold mining was important for most of the twentieth century, but diamond mining has taken precedence in the twenty-first century.

Things to keep in mind before packing up and relocating to Yellowknife:

* In June, it's hard to sleep with twenty hours of daylight; in December, it's hard to get up with five hours of daylight.

* It is the best Canadian city in which to view aurora borealis, which occurs more than two hundred days per year.

* It has a frost-free growing season of about one hundred days thanks to the moderating effect of Great Slave Lake.

Neil Young's platinum albums

* *Harvest Moon* (1997)
* *Harvest* (1994)
* *Live Rust* (1988)
* *Decade* (1986)
* *After the Gold Rush* (1986)
* *Everybody Knows This is Nowhere* (1986)
* *Rust Never Sleeps* (1979)

• • •

An Officer of the Order of Canada, *Neil Young* (1945–) is a Canadian music legend as well as an environmental and political activist. With John Mellencamp and Willie Nelson (later joined by Dave Matthews), Neil Young established Farm Aid, a non-profit organization to support family farms and sustainable agriculture. He was also, with his former wife, Pegi Young (1952–2019), a co-founder of Bridge School, an educational institution devoted to children with language and physical disabilities, and he is a strong supporter of David Suzuki's Blue Dot campaign, which seeks to include in Canada's *Charter of Rights and Freedoms* the right to live in a healthy environment.

Neil Young's music career stretches back to the mid-1960s. His major influences are country music and rhythm and blues, and his main music mentors are Bob Dylan and Elvis Presley. Young emphasizes spontaneity in his composing process, and his music includes R & B, country, folk, garage-rock, rock, and techno. Young co-founded Buffalo Springfield (Richie Furay, Dewey Martin, Bruce Palmer, Stephen Stills, Neil Young), which is credited with inventing folk-rock, and thanks to his album *Rust Never Sleeps* (1979), Young acquired the nickname "Godfather of Grunge." He has won numerous national and international music awards, and he has had a long-lasting, significant influence. He was inducted into the Rock and Roll Hall of Fame in 1995.

————————— ••• —————————

First bred in 1966, the *Yukon Gold* is a posh potato preferred by presidents, prime ministers, and princes. The Yukon Gold is the brainchild of Garnet Johnston, a researcher at the University of Guelph in Ontario. He wanted to develop a gold-fleshed potato that looked as if it were swimming in butter. The Yukon Gold potato first appeared on store shelves in 1980. Johnston did not make a penny off the potato because, at the time it was produced, plant breeders in Canada did not have intellectual property rights.

————————— ••• —————————

Z

Z IS FOR ZED,
    THE TWENTY-SIXTH LETTER
YANKEES SAY ZEE,
    BUT WE SAY IT BETTER

ZIRCON, ZINC, ZEHRS,
    ZEBRA CATERPILLARS,
ZEBALLOS, TIME ZONES,
    ZOUAVES, AND ZELLERS

Zed

Canadian English is a combination of British and American pronunciations and spellings. Unlike the Americans, Canadians pronounce the last letter of the English alphabet as "*zed.*"

— ••• —

Zircon occurs in igneous, metamorphic, and sedimentary rocks. Canada has large quarries in Ontario and Quebec and is a net exporter of the mineral. Zircon does not melt at very high temperatures, is very difficult to break, and resists abrasion. Truly a rock of ages, the oldest crystals discovered (in Australia) are 4.4 billion years old. In its different forms, zircon has a variety of uses. Zirconium is used to produce heat- and corrosion-resistant metal components (computer parts, specialty steel, high-performance alloys, lamp filaments). Zirconia is used as an opacifier, a whitening agent, and a pigment in ceramic and pottery glazes. Cubic zirconia is produced by heating zircon to a temperature above 2,730 degrees Celsius and is used to make synthetic gemstones and artificial diamonds. Cubic zirconia has a ranking of eight on the Mohs scale of hardness. Blue zircon is December's birthstone.

Did You Know?

Canada's zircon is hot stuff! From zircon, scientists can estimate the temperatures generated when asteroids collide with the earth. The presence of zirconia at the Mistastin Lake Crater in Labrador shows that a meteorite impact 38 million years ago caused surrounding surface rocks to reach temperatures between 2,730 and 2,760 degrees Celsius—the highest temperatures ever recorded for surface rocks in a natural environment.

— ••• —

Canada is one of the world's largest *zinc* producers, with mines and refineries in British Columbia, Manitoba, Ontario, Quebec, and New Brunswick. Zinc is also recovered from scrap galvanized metal and from used batteries. Zinc is essential for human health and has many other uses, including:

* to galvanize steel
* to produce alloys such as brass and bronze
* to make alloys for die-cast products like appliances, tools, and carburetors

- to produce dry cell batteries and roofing (rolled zinc metal)
- to produce zinc oxide for sunscreen and paints.

———————— ••• ————————

Zehrs Markets is a supermarket chain in southern Ontario. First established in 1950 by Emory Zehr of Kitchener, Ontario, it was acquired by Loblaw Companies in 1963 and has spread to Bolton, Stratford, and Windsor, Ontario. It has a mission of "Bringing More to the Table." The company guarantees freshness and it allows customers to "Taste Anything."

———————— ••• ————————

The striking, boldly coloured *zebra caterpillar* lives in the southern half of Canada and matures into a dull brown moth. It eats such garden produce as asparagus, broccoli, potato, spinach, and tomato.

———————— ••• ————————

Zeballos is a village located on the northwest coast of Vancouver Island. Named by explorer Captain Malaspina for one of his lieutenants, Ciriaco Cevallos, it was the site of a 1930s gold rush. An estimated $13 million worth of gold was transported from Zeballos. Today, Zeballos is a popular destination for fishing, tourism, and wilderness activities.

Did You Know?

The historic main street of Zeballos was literally paved with gold. Because of a lack of road fill, contractors built up the main road with high-grade ore containing gold. Years later, gold tailings were recovered by scraping the road surface.

———————— ••• ————————

Sir Sandford Fleming (1827–1915), a Canadian surveyor and engineer, is considered the father of international standard time. He proposed dividing the world into twenty-four *time zones* (each equal to 15 degrees of longitude and one hour), beginning at the Greenwich Meridian in England. Fleming's system was adopted in 1884 at the International Prime Meridian Conference in Washington, DC. Canada has six time zones (Pacific, Mountain, Central, Eastern, Atlantic, and Newfoundland). The time difference between Atlantic and Newfoundland is one half-hour.

Canada's Papal *Zouaves* came into being in the years 1868 to 1870. They were 507 young Canadian men, mostly recruited in Quebec, who enlisted in the international papal army in Rome to defend papal territory from the forces promoting Italian unification. Bishop Ignace Bourget set up a committee in Montréal to recruit educated men of upstanding moral character who would take up arms for Pope Pius IX in a grand fight for the papacy and against the moral evils of liberal thinking, freedom of speech, freedom of conscience, and the separation of church and state. After their return to Canada, the Zouaves's raison d'être was to defend with ideology the same evils in Quebec. They formed thirty-nine associations in Quebec and two in Ontario, and at their peak, the Zouaves had two thousand members. They were active in Quebec society: beginning in 1909 and continuing for decades, they formed an honour guard for priests making an annual pilgrimage to Beaupré (an act of devotion to honour Saint Anne and God at the Basilica of Saint Anne, which pilgrims believe is a site of miracles and a reliquary containing the forearm bone of the mother of Mary); from 1937 to 1992 they ran a bingo at the Parc de l'Exposition at the annual agricultural exhibition; from 1955 they made appearances at the Quebec Winter Carnival; in the 1960s they established cadet corps for transmitting Catholic values to young people; and they were an honorary escort for Pope John Paul during his 1984 visit to Quebec City. The Zouaves still exist today as a social club.

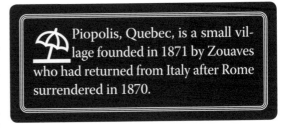

Piopolis, Quebec, is a small village founded in 1871 by Zouaves who had returned from Italy after Rome surrendered in 1870.

In 1932, Walter Zeller (1890–1957) of Kichener, Ontario, opened *Zellers* department store "for thrifty Canadians." The first stores were in southwestern Ontario, Quebec, and New Brunswick. By the 1970s, Zellers had expanded across Canada, acquiring Fields and Marshall Wells in the process. Customers could order a Big Z burger and fries in the Zellers Restaurant, fill prescriptions at the Zellers

Pharmacy, collect Club Z points for purchases, and get a free Zeddy bear if their child's birthday party was sponsored by Zellers. For twenty-five years, "The lowest price is the law" was one of the most famous slogans in Canadian retail. In 1978, the Hudson's Bay Company (HBC), wanting to expand its client base, became the sole owner of Zellers. Zellers continued to prosper as a separate division of HBC until the arrival of American companies Target and Walmart. In the twenty-first century, many Zellers stores were acquired by the now-defunct Canadian branch of Target, and the remaining two stores in Canada became discount outlets for The Bay and Home Outfitters.

— ••• —

Superlative Canada

CANADA'S FIRST

- 🍁 **bank**: The Montreal Bank, 1817
- 🍁 **hospital**: Hôtel-Dieu de Québec, 1639
- 🍁 **library (private)**: Marc Lescarbot, Port Royal, NS, 1606
- 🍁 **library (public, free tax supported)**: Saint John, NB; Guelph & Toronto, ON, 1883
- 🍁 **museum**: Barnett's Museum, Niagara Falls, ON, 1831
- 🍁 **national park**: Banff National Park, AB, 1885
- 🍁 **national urban park**: Rouge Park, Toronto, ON, 1995
- 🍁 **provincial park**: Queen Victoria Park, Niagara Falls, ON, 1885
- 🍁 **provincial park (protective)**: Algonquin Park, ON, 1893
- 🍁 **university (English)**: University of New Brunswick, 1785
- 🍁 **university (French)**: Université Laval, 1663 (Séminaire de Québec; Université Laval, 1852)

CANADA'S LARGEST

- 🍁 **city (population)**: Toronto, ON
- 🍁 **park**: Wood Buffalo National Park (44,807 km^2), AB/NWT
- 🍁 **park (city)**: North Saskatchewan River Valley Parks System (7,284 ha), Edmonton, AB
- 🍁 **island**: Baffin Island (507,451 km^2), NU
- 🍁 **freshwater island**: Manitoulin Island (2765 km^2), Lake Huron, ON
- 🍁 **lake located entirely within Canada**: Great Bear Lake (31,153 km^2), NWT

- 🍁 **Northernmost point**: Cape Columbia, Ellesmere Island, NU
- 🍁 **Southernmost point**: Middle Island, ON
- 🍁 **Easternmost point**: Cape Spear, NL
- 🍁 **Westernmost point**: Mt. St. Elias, YT

Notes

1. Statements from each astronaut (except Chris Hadfield) are direct quotations from interviews with Genna Buck and Cathy Gulli for their article "Question and Astronaut" in the August 30, 2015, issue of *Maclean's*, macleans.ca/tag/question-and-astronaut/.

2. Chris Hadfield, *An Astronaut's Guide to Life on Earth* (Toronto: Random House of Canada, 2013), 90.

3. Margaret Atwood, *Strange Things: The Malevolent North in Canadian Literature* (London: Virago, 2004), 14.

4. "Douglas Cardinal's brand of native architecture," CBC Digital Archives, September 29, 1984, cbc.ca/archives/entry/douglas-cardinals-brand-of-native-architecture.

5. "Philosophy," Douglas Cardinal Architect, djcarchitect.com/philosophy.

6. Trippy, "The World's 10 Most Beautiful Buildings," HuffPost, November 18, 2015, huffpost.com/entry/beautiful-buildings_b_8386570.

7. Tantoo Cardinal, "Voices from Native America," First Nations Drum, December 28, 2002, firstnationsdrum.com/2002/12/voices-from-native-america-by-tantoo-cardinal/.

8. Pierre Elliott Trudeau, "Exhaustion and Fulfillment: The Ascetic in a Canoe," originally published in French in *Jeunesse Etudiante Catholique*, November 1944. First published in English in *Wilderness Canada* (1970), edited by Borden Spears, canoe.ca/che-mun/102trudeau.html.

9. Mehrdad Baghai and James Quigley, "Cirque du Soleil: A Very Different Vision of Teamwork," Fast Company, February 4, 2011, fastcompany.com/1724123/cirque-du-soleil-very-different-vision-teamwork.

10. Leonard Cohen's acceptance speech, "Leonard Cohen is inducted into the Canadian Songwriters

Hall of Fame (CSHF)," YouTube, November 19, 2015, youtube.com/watch?v=Pq3tMW65t60.

11. Lord Durham quoted in "Durham Report," The Canadian Encyclopedia, thecanadianencyclopedia.ca/en/article/durham-report/.

12. Hugh John Macdonald quoted in "Passage of an era" (plaque), Kakabeka Falls Provincial Park, Government of Ontario.

13. Alison Northcott, "Last surviving Dionne quintuplets hope to preserve family home," CBC News, May 25, 2017, cbc.ca/news/canada/montreal/dionne-quintuplets-north-bay-1.4128021.

14. Quoted in Russell Bingham, "Viola Desmond," The Canadian Encyclopedia, January 27, 2013, the-canadianencyclopedia.ca/en/article/viola-desmond.

15. Elaine Gold, "Canadian, Eh?: A Survey of Contemporary Use" (PDF): 2, University of Toronto, Queen's University, homes.chass.utoronto.ca/~cla-acl/actes2004/Gold-CLA-2004.pdf.

16. "The Vision," Idle No More, idlenomore.ca.

17. "1929: Women Become Persons," CBC Digital Archives, June 11, 1938, cbc.ca/archives/entry/1929-women-become-persons.

18. Greenpeace poster: "When the last tree is cut, the last river poisoned, and the last fish dead, we will discover that we can't eat money....," accessed through a Google search.

19. Lee J. Sanders, "From Thebes to Toronto and the 21st Century: An Incredible Journey," Diabetes Spectrum, January 2002, spectrum.diabetesjournals.org/content/15/1/56.

20. *Kakabeka Falls 2016 Information Guide*, Ontario Parks, Queens Printer for Ontario, ca. 2016.

21. "The Legend of Greenmantle" (plaque), Kakabeka Falls Provincial Park, Government of Ontario.

22. Chief Dan George quoted in "Native American Wisdom," Inspiration for the Spirit, inspirationforthespirit.com/native-american-wisdom/.

23. Sir Wilfrid Laurier quoted in "Statement of the Prime Minister of

Canada on the establishment of the Office of Religious Freedom," Prime Minister Stephen Harper, Government of Canada, February 20, 2013, canada.ca/en/news/archive/2013/02/statement-prime-minister-canada-establishment-office-religious-freedom.html.

24. Christopher Hume, "When Norval Morriseau talks, others listen; where he goes, disciples follow," *Maclean's*, January 22, 1979, macleans.ca/archives/when-norval-morrisseau-talks-others-listen-where-he-goes-disciples-follow/.

25. Joyce Hardcastle, "Nanaimo Bar Recipe," City of Nanaimo, ca. 2017, nanaimo.ca/EN/main/visitors/NanaimoBars.html. Reprinted with permission from the City of Nanaimo.

26. Peter Narvaez, "The Folklore of 'Old Foolishness': Newfoundland Media Legends," (PDF): 134, canlit.ca/article/the-folklore-of-old-foolishness-2/.

27. Donald J. C. Phillipson, "Reginald Fessenden," The Canadian Encyclopedia, updated March 4, 2015, thecanadianencyclopedia.ca/en/article/reginald-fessenden.

28. Laura Neilson Bonikowsky, "Laura Secord," The Canadian Encyclopedia, updated March 24, 2015, thecanadianencyclopedia.ca/en/article/laura-secord.

29. "Tim Hortons Kandahar Deployment Comes to an End," Tim Hortons.com, November 24, 2011, timhortons.com/ca/en/corporate/news-release.php?id=7619.

30. Wendy Hayward quoted in "Afghan Tim Hortons Closure End of an Era," CTV News, November 28, 2011, ctvnews.ca/afghan-tim-hortons-closure-end-of-an-era-1.732570.

31. Mark Kuhlberg, "Lumberjacks," The Canadian Encyclopedia, updated April 16, 2015, thecanadianencyclopedia.ca/en/article/lumberjacks.

32. Laura Neilson Bonikowsky, "Alexander Graham Bell and the Invention of the Telephone," The Canadian Encyclopedia, updated March 4, 2015, thecanadianencyclopedia.ca/en/article/whats-better-than-bells-telephone-feature/.

33. Chief Rose Laboucan, "Treaties are the Foundation of Canada," ATA Magazine 89, 4, 2008–2009,

The Alberta Teachers' Association, teachers.ab.ca/News%20Room/ata%20magazine/Volume%2089/Number4/Articles/Pages/TreatiesaretheFoundationofCanada.aspx.

34. Isabelle Montpetit, "Treaties from 1760–1923: Two sides to the story," CBC News, updated July 13, 2011, cbc.ca/news/canada/treaties-from-1760-1923-two-sides-to-the-story-1.1081839.

35. Chief Poundmaker quoted in "The Story of Treaty Six: Negotiations Continue (1876)," Treaty 6 Education, treaty6education.lskysd.ca/negotiations.html.

36. Georges-Philéas Vanier quoted in "Governor General The Right Honourable Georges Philias Vanier," The Office of the Governor General of Canada, archive.gg.ca/gg/fgg/bios/01/vanier_e.asp.

37. Jean Vanier, *Becoming Human* (Toronto: House of Anansi Press, 1998), 82–83.

38. A. E. Ross quoted by Anthony Wilson-Smith in "Vimy Ridge," The Canadian Encyclopedia, thecanadianencyclopedia.ca/en/article/vimy-ridge-and-the-birth-of-a-nation/.

Appendix 1

CANADIAN PROVINCES AND THEIR OFFICIAL SYMBOLS AND EMBLEMS

PROVINCE OR TERRITORY	FLORAL EMBLEM	OFFICIAL BIRD	OFFICIAL MINERAL/ GEMSTONE	OFFICIAL TREE	OFFICIAL/ HERITAGE ANIMAL
ALBERTA	wild rose	great horned owl	petrified wood	lodgepole pine	Rocky Mt. big-horn sheep
BRITISH COLUMBIA	Pacific dogwood	Stellar's jay	jade	Western red cedar	kermode bear (spirit bear)
MANITOBA	prairie crocus	great grey owl	❋	white spruce	plains bison
NEW BRUNSWICK	purple violet	black-capped chickadee	Holmesville Soil Series (official soil)	balsam fir	❋
NEWFOUNDLAND AND LABRADOR	pitcher plant	Atlantic puffin	labradorite	black spruce	Newfoundland pony
NORTHWEST TERRITORIES	mountain avens	gyrfalcon	diamond	tamarack/larch	Arctic grayling (official fish)
NOVA SCOTIA	trailing arbutus (mayflower)	osprey	stillbite/agate	red spruce	Nova Scotia duck tolling retriever / Sable Island horse
NUNAVUT	purple saxifrage	aqiggiq (rock ptarmigan)	❋	❋	qimmiq (Canadian Inuit dog)
ONTARIO	white trillium	common loon	amethyst	Eastern white pine	❋
PRINCE EDWARD ISLAND	lady's slipper	blue jay	Charlottetown Soil Series (official soil)	red oak	❋
QUEBEC	blue flag	snowy owl	❋	yellow birch	
SASKATCHEWAN	Western red lily	sharp-tailed grouse	potash	white birch	white-tailed deer
YUKON	fireweed	raven	lazulite	subalpine fir	

Appendix II

NATIONAL PARKS, NATIONAL PARK RESERVES (NPR), AND NATIONAL MARINE CONSERVATION AREAS (NMCA) OF CANADA

PROVINCE	NATIONAL PARK/RESERVE/MARINE CONSERVATION AREA	YEAR ESTABLISHED	AREA (SQ KM)
ALBERTA	Banff	1885	6,641
	Elk Island	1913	194
	Jasper	1907	10,878
	Waterton Lakes	1895	505
ALBERTA & NORTHWEST TERRITORIES	Wood Buffalo	1922	44,802
BRITISH COLUMBIA	Glacier	1886	1,349.3
	Gulf Islands NPR	2010	36 (land)
	Gwaii Hanaas NPR, NMCA Reserve, Haida Heritage Site	1993	1,495
	Kootenay	1920	1,406.4
	Mount Revelstoke	1914	259.7
	Pacific Rim NPR	2001	285.8 (land)
	South Okanagan-Similkameen NPR (memorandum of understanding)	2019	273
	Yoho	1886	1,313.1
MANITOBA	Riding Mountain	1929	2,973.1
	Wapusk	1996	11,475
NEW BRUNSWICK	Fundy	1948	205.9
	Kouchibouguak	1979	239.2

PROVINCE	NATIONAL PARK/RESERVE/MARINE CONSERVATION AREA	YEAR ESTABLISHED	AREA (SQ KM)
NEWFOUNDLAND & LABRADOR	Akami-Uapishkᵁ-KakKasuak-Mealy Mountains NPR	2015	10,700
	Gros Morne	1970	1,805
	Terra Nova	1957	399.9
	Torngat Mountains	2008	9,700
NORTHWEST TERRITORIES	Aulavik	1992	12,200
	Nááts'ihch'oh NPR	2012	4,850
	Nahanni NPR	1976	30,000
	Thaidene Nene NPR	2019	14,000
	Tuktut Nogait	1998	18,181
NOVA SCOTIA	Cape Breton Highlands	1936	948
	Kejimkujik	1974	403.7
	Sable Island NPR	2011	34
NUNAVUT	Auyuittuq	2001	19,089
	Qausuittuq	2015	11,000
	Quttinirpaaq	1988	37,775
	Sirmilik	1999	22,252
	Ukkusiksalik	2003	20,500

PROVINCE	NATIONAL PARK/RESERVE/MARINE CONSERVATION AREA	YEAR ESTABLISHED	AREA (SQ KM)
ONTARIO	Bruce Peninsula	1987	156
	Fathom Five National Marine Park	1987	113
	Georgian Bay Islands	1929	25.6
	Lake Superior NMCA	2007	10,850
	Point Pelee	1918	15
	Pukaskwa	1978	1,877.8
	Rouge National Urban Park	2015	79.1
	Thousand Islands	1914	24
PRINCE EDWARD ISLAND	Prince Edward Island	1937	21.5
QUEBEC	Forillon	1974	240.4
	La Mauricie	1970	536.1
	Mingan Archipelago NPR	1984	150.7
	Saguenay–St. Lawrence Marine Park	1998	1138
SASKATCHEWAN	Grasslands	1981	906.4
	Prince Albert	1927	3,874.3
YUKON	Ivvavik	1984	9,750
	Kluane NP and Reserve	1976	22,013.3
	Vuntut	1995	4,345

Selected Bibliography

ELECTRONIC RESOURCES

Canada History
canadahistory.com

Canada Post
canadapost.ca

Canada's First Peoples
firstpeoplesofcanada.com

Canada's History
canadashistory.ca

Canada's Sports Hall of Fame
sportshall.ca

Canadian Broadcasting Corporation
cbc.ca

The Canadian Canoe Museum
canoemuseum.ca

The Canadian Encyclopedia
thecanadianencyclopedia.ca

Canadian Geographic
canadiangeographic.ca

Canadian Heritage
canada.ca/en/canadian-heritage

Canadian Museum of History
historymuseum.ca

Canadian Songwriters Hall of Fame
cshf.ca

Canadian Theatre Encyclopedia
canadiantheatre.com

CBC Books
cbc.ca/books

CBC Digital Archives
cbc.ca/archives

CBC News
cbc.ca/news

CTV News
ctvnews.ca

Daily Hive
dailyhive.com

Dictionary of Canadian Biography
biographi.ca

Encyclopaedia Britannica
britannica.com

Environment and Natural Resources:
canada.ca/en/services/environment

First Nations Drum
firstnationsdrum.com

The Globe and Mail
theglobeandmail.com

Government of Canada
canada.ca

Government of Ontario
ontario.ca/page/government-ontario)

Historica Canada
historicacanada.ca

Huffington Post
huffingtonpost.ca

IndigenousPeople.net
indigenouspeople.net

Ingenium Canada
ingeniumcanada.org

Inventive Kids
inventivekids.com

Journey North
journeynorth.org

L'Encyclopédie de l'histoire du Québec/The Quebec History Encyclopedia
faculty.marianopolis.edu/c.belanger/quebechistory/encyclopedia

Library and Archives Canada
collectionscanada.gc.ca

Live Science
livescience.com

Maclean's
macleans.ca

National Capital Commission
ncc-ccn.gc.ca

National Film Board of Canada
nfb.ca

National Geographic

nationalgeographic.com

National Post

news.nationalpost.com

Native Languages of the Americas

native-languages.org

Parks Canada

pc.gc.ca

RIAA

riaa.com

ThoughtCo

thoughtco.com

Toronto Star

thestar.com

Torontoist

torontoist.com

Vancouver Sun

vancouversun.com

PRINT RESOURCES

Atwood, Margaret. *Strange Things: The Malevolent North in Canadian Literature.* London: Virago, 2004.

Hadfield, Chris. *An Astronaut's Guide to Life on Earth.* Toronto: Random House of Canada, 2013.

Ipellie, Alootook and David Macdonald. *The Inuit Thought of It: Amazing Arctic Innovations.* Toronto: Annick Press, 2007.

MacGregor, Roy. *Canoe Country: The Making of Canada.* Toronto: Random House, 2015.

McQuarrie, Neil. *The Forgotten Trail: From Prince Arthur's Landing to Red River.* Brandon: NJM Enterprises, 2013.

Neuzil, Mark and Norman Sims. *Canoes: A Natural History in North America.* Minneapolis: University of Minnesota Press, 2016.

Rayburn, Alan. *Naming Canada: Stories about Canadian Place Names,* rev. ed. Toronto: University of Toronto Press, 2001.

———. *Place Names of Canada.* 2nd ed. Oxford: Oxford University Press, 2010.

Rose, Alex. *Who Killed the Grand Banks: The Untold Story Behind the Decimation of One of the World's Greatest Natural Resources.* Mississauga: John Wiley & Sons, 2008.

Ruffo, Armand Garnet. *Norval Morrisseau: Man Changing into Thunderbird.* Madeira Park, BC: Douglas and McIntyre, 2013.